VALUOCITY

A Fable for Dentists

Other Books by Dr. Marc Cooper:

Mastering the Business of Practice

*Partnerships in Dental Practice:
Why Some Succeed and Why Some Fail*

*SOURCE: The Genesis of
Success in Business and Life*

*Running on Empty
Answers to Questions Dentists have
about the Recession
(with Christopher Creamer)*

VALUOCITY

A Fable for Dentists

BY

DR. MARC B. COOPER

DR. MARK E. SILBERG

The Mastery Company
Woodinville, Washington

VALUOCITY
A Fable for Dentists

Text Copyright © 2009 by
Dr. Marc B. Cooper and Dr. Mark E. Silberg
All Rights Reserved.

Published by Sahalie Press
Woodinville, Washington
(425) 806-8830
info@masterycompany.com

No part of this publication may be reproduced in whole or in part, or stored in a retrieval system, or transmitted in any form or by any means, electronic, mechanical, photocopying, recording or otherwise, without permission in writing from Sahalie Press, except by a reviewer who may quote brief passages in a review. For longer quotations, permission requests may be addressed to: Sahalie Press, PO Box 1806, Woodinville, WA 98072, USA

ISBN: 978-0-9763584-7-3

Library of Congress Control Number: 2009936777

Printed in the U.S.A.

First Edition, 2009

Editing by Matthew King

Book design by Lightbourne, Inc.

DEDICATION

We are dedicating this book to our fellow dentists who have trusted to share their professional and personal lives with us.

You have directly contributed to our respective professional success and our growth as human beings.

This book is our thanks to you.

ACKNOWLEDGEMENTS

We wish to acknowledge the people who have contributed so much to this book.

Our primary relationships, Lisa and Sally, extraordinary women who hold us to our highest thoughts and uppermost integrity. Thank you for your commitment, love and support.

Our children, Kory, Sam, Max, Ami and Ali, who keep the future present and continually ground us in reality.

Our parents, Sid and Sadie Cooper and Julius and Lillian Silberg, who sacrificed and dedicated their lives so we could make our own lives extraordinary.

Our staffs of dedicated people whose work and commitment allow us to fulfill our vision.

Our publisher, Chris Creamer, whose talent, hard work and core value of excellence made this book possible.

Our editor, Matt King, who works to bring our ideas both clarity and consistency.

Our designer, Shannon Bodie, and the folks at Lightbourne, for their incredible talent in cover design and layout and their enduring partnership.

And to all those dental professionals committed to helping dentists be all they can be.

CONTENTS

A Rock and a Hard Place	1
Fresh Air	5
Veronica	10
The Floodgates Open	15
The Teacher Appears	22
The Chicken or the Truth	29
Road to the Ranch	35
Fierce Eagle and Failing Mouse	39
The Payoff	42
Homework Aha	46
The Challenge	49
Surrender	57
A Question of Excellence	59
To the Core	69
Taking a Stand	73
No Free Lunch	79
Owning up to Upsets	82
Behave Yourself	85
Refine to Define	89
Measure. Measure. Measure.	94
Request for the Best	98
Ranch Style	104

You Can't Go Back	110
Afraid of Commitment	113
Take Off the Training Wheels	121
Hope, Prayer & Job Descriptions	127
Choosing and Losing (or Winning)	131
Hold to Account	135
In the Bucket	140
The Value of Values	145
Do I Get Paid for This?	149
Ready to Perform	155
Beer View Mirror	162
Practice Success	164
Raising the Stakes	171
Put me in Coach	178
Pay Back to Move Forward	181
Homeward Bound	183
About the Authors	186
Taos Pueblo	188
Introduction to Valuocity II	189

VALUOCITY

A Fable for Dentists

ONE

A Rock and a Hard Place

THE BRIGHT LIGHTS STARTLED HIM. Carl blinked out of his trance, suddenly aware that he was sitting among 350 dentists in a large room at the San Antonio Convention Center. He was attending a three hour presentation on restoring implants being given by a highly regarded clinician from Seattle. But he hadn't heard a single word. Even the images on the PowerPoint slides hadn't registered; they were nothing but a fleeting montage of teeth, porcelain, bone, blood and metal. Carl had been in another world.

During the implant presentation, he had been fast-forwarding through his life, trying to understand how he'd come so far professionally — and, yet, was so close to losing it all. Carl Oldquist was a 49-year old general dentist in his 14th year of practice. He'd graduated from Case Western Reserve, spent two years in the Air Force and then completed a General Practice residency. He had worked as an associate in Milwaukee for two years with the intention of purchasing the practice after a short partnership, but the deal had fallen through.

That experience prompted Carl to purchase his own practice in Madison, on Mound Street close to Meriter Hospital. He upgraded the office: new chairs, new delivery systems, new floors, new lighting — the whole nine-yards. It was a very functional space of 2100 square feet with five operatories. Carl signed a 10-year lease and received some needed lease-hold dollars from the owner.

Over the ensuing 13 years, the practice grew in active and recall patients, in revenues, in technologies and materials, and in the kind of dentistry he could provide. Carl considered himself a CE junkie. He loved to learn and get technically better. He studied with the masters: Pankey, Spears and Kois. Simply put, he was a strong clinician and he loved his dentistry.

Carl was no slacker in practice management either. He attended programs regularly, participated in a study club, read bestselling business books and hired highly regarded consultants to help improve practice performance and refine practice systems and structures. He also invested in developing his staff. By 2007, Carl had a solid million dollar practice with one full-time and one part-time hygienist, two assistants, two front desks and a part-time sterilization assistant.

Personally, he was happily married, had two teenagers and a very nice Tudor style home on a corner lot. His interest in cars kept his four car garage full with some very sweet rides — a Silver 1999 Porsche 911, a navy blue 2005 Mercedes S500, a bright red, fully restored 1964 Dodge pickup, and, of course, the family car, a 2006 Acura SUV. He didn't want his kids driving any of these cars so there was a used 2003 Honda Civic sitting in the driveway for his son Jonathan to drive. His youngest, Amy, wouldn't be driving for two more years. With his family and practice Carl felt he should consider himself a very fortunate man, but recently he felt anything but lucky.

In spite of the outward appearances of financial success, over the last year Carl had been experiencing a severe slowdown as the global financial meltdown crept into his practice. New patient numbers had shrunk from about 22 a month to less than 10. Cancellations and no-shows in hygiene were up over 40%. His columns had plenty of holes. Worse, the new patients he had, and even those coming out of recall, were delaying or declining more lucrative treatments.

As he became aware of the declining numbers in his practice, Carl had applied all the things he'd learned about practice management. Regular staff meetings, more broadcast marketing with brochures and a newsletter, upgrading his website, asking patients to refer other patients, combing recall patient charts for undone restorative work, confirming patients twice. You name it, he was doing it. But last month was so bad, he couldn't make payroll. Carl had to execute a line of credit with his bank to cover expenses. He'd started taking home a reduced salary. Worse, when he looked at the book for next month, it was a total disaster. Nothing was working and his bottom line was in freefall.

And that's the dismal world Carl had disappeared to when the conference room lights went out, the slides lit up and the speaker began his presentation. Carl's mind was consumed with worry, fear and trepidation about the future of his practice — and his family. *What am I going to do? What if I can't make it? What if the economic situation gets worse? What if I fail?*

Now that the lights had come back on and the crowd around him began to stir, Carl was jolted back to the present. He was at this ADA conference to learn what to do so those questions of failure didn't nag at him. But as he sat there, knowing that his practice was sandwiched between a rock and a hard place made his decision to come to this conference appear desperate.

As his fellow dentists began to exit, Carl stayed pressed to his seat as if a great weight, a terrible mountain of doubt, prevented him from rising.

TWO

Fresh Air

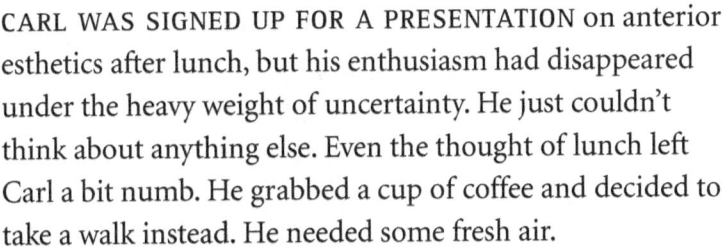

CARL WAS SIGNED UP FOR A PRESENTATION on anterior esthetics after lunch, but his enthusiasm had disappeared under the heavy weight of uncertainty. He just couldn't think about anything else. Even the thought of lunch left Carl a bit numb. He grabbed a cup of coffee and decided to take a walk instead. He needed some fresh air.

Making his way out of the convention center, he was hailed by some colleagues to join them for lunch, but he waved absently back and called out that he had an appointment. *An appointment?* he thought. *I'm going nowhere — and fast.* With a muted sigh, he slung his black ADA conference bag over his shoulder and headed out into the bright sunshine and emerging heat of the day.

Carl had been to San Antonio a few times before and knew his way around town. He headed west on Market Street and soon found himself on a stairway descending to the River Walk. It was warm, certainly a change from Madison this time of year. But rather than enjoying the change in climate, Carl was deep in thought. *What do I need to do to pull my practice out of this mess? I've tried everything I know and nothing has worked. What's going to happen to my family if I fail?*

As Carl walked along the River Walk he was too preoccupied with his thoughts to notice other strollers or the towering cypress trees. He failed to smell the spicy aromas wafting from the Mexican cafes along the river. He was deaf to the tour guides on barges weaving their stories of the Alamo and old San Antonio. All he could register was the unending refrain playing in his muddled head: *What am I going to do?*

His situation felt hopeless. His practice was circling the drain and he had no answers. To make matters worse, here he was at the ADA meeting, surrounded by people with possible solutions, and he couldn't bring himself to ask for help. He wasn't even sure what he'd ask for.

At a bend in the river, he glanced at his watch. Almost an hour had passed and his thoughts were no clearer. The stroll had brought him no respite, or inspiration. He considered going back to the convention center, but the thought of sitting in a dark room with hundreds of dentists, watching presentations about advanced dentistry he wasn't able to provide since patients weren't buying, chatting with his peers and pretending everything was fine, seemed ludicrous.

A wave of fatigue overtook Carl. He found a nearby bench under a sprawling Magnolia tree and sat down. He stared vacantly at the river, his mind fixated on his floundering practice. He just couldn't work out how to reignite his business, how to get new patients through the door, how to get his patients to accept treatment, how to motivate his staff to pull together and make it work.

His thoughts turned to his wife, Veronica, and their two children. Their whole life style was being threatened. Not only because of the downturn in his practice, but also because recent losses in the stock market had evaporated his retirement fund. All the years he had put into building his practice and creating a secure future for his family were on the brink. The question *What am I going to do?* pounded like a pulse on his overloaded brain.

Carl, consumed with worry, didn't notice when an elderly gentleman sat down next to him on the bench. Oblivious to everyone and everything, Carl stared blankly.

"Carl, you don't look so good," the older man said matter of factly.

Carl snapped out of his fog and turned to the man seated next to him, trying to register the face. Did he know him? If he didn't, how had this stranger known his name?

"Excuse me?" Carl said, buying time. He couldn't think of how he knew the man seated next to him or vice versa. But then Carl realized the stranger had an ADA name tag on a lanyard around his neck. Carl was still wearing his own name tag which read: Carl Oldquist, DDS, Madison WI, General Practice.

Carl took a good look at the older gentleman. He was slim with thin white hair, a goatee and mustache. At first glance, he struck Carl as a slender version of Colonel Sanders, but with a certain air of gravitas. He looked grandfatherly and kind, but not comical. He wore an off-white suit, a white shirt and a bolo.

Before Carl could read his name tag, the old man introduced himself. "My name is Sidney Kaprov. I didn't mean to disturb you, but you look a little troubled. You look like you could use someone to talk to."

Carl thought a moment about this scene: here he was hundreds of miles from home sitting by a river in Texas and out of nowhere a white-suited man appears like some character right out of a B-movie asking if he can be of service. An angelic Colonel Sanders trying to earn his wings — and not chicken wings. Just what Carl needed. He'd left the conference to get away from his problems, and now some amateur do-gooder was trying to choke off his last breath of privacy.

"I'm fine." Carl smiled, but his tone said *Mind your own business.*

"Well," replied Sidney, "your frown is sending a very different message. You look plenty troubled to me. I thought maybe I could help. I'm not in the habit of butting into a person's private affairs, but I noticed your ADA name tag, and I have a great deal of experience with dental practices. I do consulting work."

Carl didn't know what to say. He wasn't in the habit of talking about his practice with others, except with consultants he'd hired when his practice had been growing rapidly. His business was a private matter, especially now that the practice was in rapid decline.

"No, I'm fine, really. Thanks for asking," Carl said, hoping to put an end to the matter.

Sidney took out his wallet. "Carl, here's my card just in case you need to talk to someone. I know dentists don't like to talk to other dentists about their problems, but I have helped a few dentists through tough times, and the dental industry is definitely in tough times."

Carl took the business card and looked it over with a pale grin.

VALUOCITY
You Can't Fail When You Base Your Practice on Your Values

Dr. Sidney Kaprov
General Dentistry & Practice Counselor
PO Box 1806
Taos, NM 87577
www.Valuocity.org

SydneyK@Valuocity.org
Ph. 505 488-7479 – Cell 505 890-4889

The Slogan, *You Can't Fail When You Base Your Practice on Your Values,* made no immediate impression on Carl, and he automatically slipped the card into his jacket pocket. He responded with a polite, though curt, thank you to Sidney and then rose quickly, heading back in the direction of the Marriott where he was staying.

As he walked, Carl couldn't get Sidney out of his mind. It was an unusual encounter. Yet, there was something about him — something about his demeanor, his smile, the sense of understanding he conveyed. *Definitely a well-meaning individual,* Carl thought, *but I've got to manage things for myself and make it work.*

He took a deep breath and sighed heavily. The air felt somewhat crisper now, like the wind had changed directions. Carl, with his head down, barely noticed it.

THREE

Veronica

WHEN CARL ARRIVED AT HIS HOTEL ROOM, he was greeted by the cool rush of air conditioning. It felt good. He was perspiring slightly from the walk back. His mind was still racing; the meeting with Sidney continued to replay in his head. He took the business card out of his pocket and read it again. VALUOCITY: *You Can't Fail When You Base Your Practice on Your Values.* Carl still couldn't grasp the meaning. He tossed the card down by the hotel phone.

Seeing the telephone, he remembered he'd been running late that morning and hadn't called home. Carl got out his cell phone and turned it on. As he pressed the speed dial for his home number, his thoughts turned to Veronica.

They'd been married for 17 years. He'd met Veronica while he was a junior in dental school and she was completing her Masters in sociology. Veronica's older brother was in Carl's class and he'd introduced them.

They hit it off immediately. They got married at the end of Carl's senior year and Veronica joined him on his first Air Force assignment in Minot, North Dakota where she promptly became pregnant with Jonathan. By the time Carl completed his GPR in Chicago, Jonathan was three and their daughter, Amy, was almost a year old.

While Carl was an associate, Veronica stayed home with the kids. But when Carl purchased the Madison practice, she dug in and really helped him build the business. She did the payables, payroll, helped with office design, hosted a few practice open houses, joined the wives' club of the local dental society and was the perfect support Carl needed. Carl openly discussed all the issues and problems he was encountering in his first years of practice and Veronica provided him with sage advice. He and Veronica were a dynamic team. He trusted her judgment and she had excellent people skills.

After five years of practice, the money had become predictable and the concern about Carl making it had disappeared. Although Carl and Veronica talked about the practice every day, the details, the personnel issues, the problems and the technical advancements became less a part of those conversations. Long before his tenth year in practice, the conversations had evolved into light check-ins, or gossip about staff and other dentists.

When Carl started feeling the effects of the downturn, he didn't know quite how to bring it up with Veronica. Thinking it would pass quickly, he simply didn't say anything except that he was taking a smaller salary for a couple of months to pay a bigger bite on the digital x-ray he'd purchased. But as time went on, and business didn't turn around, he became afraid to tell Veronica. And because he'd kept the bad news from her, she had no idea what was going on.

As Carl waited for the home phone to ring back in Madison, he felt shame and embarrassment for not having confided in his wife. She had sacrificed and worked hard to build the practice as much as he had. He just didn't know how to tell her.

How was he supposed to tell Veronica that they might be mere months away from a financial collapse? That soon they'd have to take money out of their retirement accounts to pay the bills. That they'd need to stop spending so much, give up the country club, stop going to the gym, sell a car or two. That she would probably have to go back to work so they could pay the mortgage.

Carl didn't know where or how to begin, so he hadn't said anything. He'd pretended everything was fine. All the same, she'd begun to notice the stress. Whenever she'd ask how things were going, he'd tell her he was busy, but that, overall, things were fine. He rationalized his evasive responses, convincing himself there was no need to worry her.

But as the situation deteriorated and the pressure grew, he began distancing himself from Veronica. And the more she asked, the more reserved and isolated he became. She began to think Carl's distance had something to do with their marriage. It was a vicious cycle. Not only was his practice going down the tube, their relationship was following close behind.

As the phone rang, Carl hoped he would get voicemail, but on the fourth ring, a breathless Veronica answered.

"Hi honey, how's the meeting? Glad you caught me. I just got back from playing tennis with Nikki. I've still got to get Amy from soccer practice and then we're meeting up with Jonathon for pizza after his Aikido class."

It sounded rushed, like she was in a hurry. What could he say to her now? So, like always, he didn't say much of anything.

"The meeting's fine so far. I went to the lecture on implants this morning, another on new materials. And I had a beer with Sam Sherman who sends his regards. How are the kids?"

"Fine. They're wondering when you'll be back and if you'll notice if they drive one of your precious cars." Veronica laughed. A sound that made Carl feel both better and worse at the same time.

"I'm landing around seven on Thursday, so I should be home by eight. Tell them I'm going to check the odometers first thing," he said, trying to mimic her lightheartedness.

"Great, honey. I'll let them know how much you *car* — I mean, *care* — about them. Alright, I gotta go. Talk to you later. Love you. Bye Bye."

"Bye, sweetie, I'll check in tomorrow," Carl said and flipped his phone shut.

Two ships passing in the night, Carl thought. *But, I don't want to get her crazy with what's going on. If I tell her how deep the trouble is, she'll just worry. I'll be able to handle this.*

Yet Carl knew it was foolish to hope for a financial turnaround in the next few months. Hope was a terrible business plan. His mind turned back to the nagging questions that had dogged him for months. *What am I going to do? What if my practice doesn't turn around? What if I go belly-up? Would Veronica stick with me?*

FOUR

The Floodgates Open

AFTER HE HUNG UP WITH VERONICA, Carl turned on his laptop to connect to the office computer and check the numbers. His heart sank. New patients were dismal, only four on the books. Receivables were growing. His schedule for the rest of the month was riddled with holes. And to make matters worse, the only highlights were single fillings and a couple of crowns.

He only had one implant case that could be ready to go this month. Six months ago, he would have had four, maybe five large implant cases in process and a crown or two every day. His daily target used to be $7,000 which he usually made. Now he was lucky to bring in half that. A pang of despair engulfed him.

Then another empty feeling crept into his gut. He was hungry. It was late afternoon, and he hadn't eaten anything since breakfast. In his current state of mind, Carl didn't feel like going out, so he called room service. As he ordered, Carl found himself staring at the business card he'd dropped on the desk. He picked up it up, slowly fingering the edges.

He had used many consultants over the years, but they all told him basically the same thing: Do more and do it better. More of the same thing. The problem for Carl was the same thing wasn't working anymore!

Why do more of the same, when it isn't working, he thought. Was Sidney Kaprov just another consultant ready to take his money for more of the same? He'd never know unless he called, but Carl hesitated. *I can't just call him. I don't even know him. I don't know anything about him.*

Still, Carl felt desperate. He needed some kind of plan, some kind of help to stop the bleeding. He glanced at his watch. It was almost 5 PM. Sidney would most likely be heading out for dinner. That let him off the hook. He'd wait until around 9 PM to call him — if he'd call him at all.

Carl changed his clothes and turned on ESPN to get his mind off his situation. His food arrived twenty minutes later: tomato bisque, club sandwich and a Heineken. Carl was glad to see the food, but got upset when he was handed a bill for $36. Money was so tight. The room service bill was just another reminder of how broke he felt and how much he couldn't afford. Last year he wouldn't have given it a thought. Now, $36 for soup and a sandwich seemed outrageous.

He hadn't had to worry about money for years. The practice had grown steadily at 12 to 15% a year. He'd been so busy that access used to be his major problem. A year ago he didn't have an open restorative appointment for eight weeks, now it was less than a day or two. Hygiene used to be booked tightly. These days, hygiene cancellations couldn't be filled.

Until recently, prosperity and abundance was all he'd known. In fact, just a year ago, Carl considered investing in his own building and increasing the footprint to 5,200 square feet, taking on an associate and increasing hygiene. Now he didn't know if he could make next month's rent.

And Carl hadn't been reckless with his money. He'd been putting away $40K a year for his retirement the last nine years and had socked away a decent amount in a 529 College Savings Plans. He had his money with a financial group out of Southern California. Less than a year ago, his financial advisor had assured him, "You're right on the path to financial freedom. The way your fee-for-service market is growing, you'll be able to comfortably retire by your late 50s or early 60's. Just keep on writing those checks."

Currently, he was way down in his 401K and his IRA, the 529s not quite as much. But forget about Ivy League universities for the kids; it was state schools now, with student loans.

Carl finished his soup and sandwich, then drained the beer. The meal was tasty, though the $36 price still left a bitter aftertaste. He just couldn't see any positives at the moment. He slumped onto the bed and changed channels to the news. Not a good idea. Unemployment numbers were up, economic indicators down. Sluggish growth predicted for many months, maybe years. Not what Carl needed right now. He closed his eyes and let out a deep breath.

Surprisingly, he fell asleep quickly. Unfortunately for

Carl, his dreams were nightmarish. He stood at the base of a mammoth concrete structure, like Hoover Dam. Veronica, Jonathon and Amy were at the top waving to him. But Carl could see cracks starting to form in the dam. Quickly, the cracks spread.

Carl tried shouting to his family, but he couldn't move or speak. It was as if he were cemented in place. The cracks grew larger. Carl looked around for something to stop the cracks from spreading. The space around him was empty. He was alone.

Then, from the corner of his eye, he caught a flash of white. He looked to the side of the dam's giant spillway where a figure sat on a bench waving. A figure all in white. Carl wanted to wave back, but he still couldn't move.

Above him, he heard mechanical grinding as the iron floodgates on the spillway began to open. The man in white got up and stood on the bench, waving as a frothing torrent of water headed down the spillway. Directly in the torrent's path, Carl strained to move his feet. Desperately he pulled, and quite suddenly he lurched forward a step.

The lurch woke Carl. For a moment he was disoriented. Then he saw a weatherman on the television. He was back in his Marriott room, not about to be swept away by the floodwaters of a failing dam. He looked over at the clock on the night stand. 9:10. He clicked off the television, got up and washed his face to help him back into the waking world.

He sat down at the small desk and stared at Sidney's card. He picked up his cell and began to dial the number. He stopped. *What am I going to say to him? Calling a stranger to help rescue my practice? How is this going to make a difference? Am I really this desperate?*

He stared in the mirror above the desk, hair wildly askew, his face pale and deep circles under his eyes. *Yeah,* he had to admit, *I look pretty desperate.*

He dialed.

After the first ring, Carl thought about hanging up. After the second ring, Carl got nervous about what he would say if Sidney answered. After the third ring, Carl almost did hang up. Then, in the middle of the fourth ring, Sidney answered with a soft-spoken "Hello?"

"Sorry to call so late," Carl said apologetically. "It's Carl, the guy you met on the River Walk today."

"It's not that late, Carl. Glad you called. Actually, I half expected you would."

Carl felt an odd sense of relief. He felt welcomed and this put him at ease.

Sidney continued, "I know how difficult it may have been for you to make this call. We dentists don't like to ask for help. We'll pay for practice consultants, but we'll rarely ask our colleagues for help or advice."

"Yeah," Carl agreed, "I've called my previous consultants about the situation, but all I got was more of the same advice. And even though I'm following it, nothing is working."

There was a long pause, and then Sidney asked, "Carl, are you open enough to tell me what's going on with you and your practice?"

Though he'd called Sidney for help, Carl didn't want

to sound like a loser. He hesitated to share the mess his practice was in and what it might mean for his marriage and family.

Sidney responded to Carl's hesitation like a mind reader. "You're probably uncertain whether to tell me about the nitty gritty of your situation. I imagine you're concerned about what I'll think about you. Nobody wants to look bad or incompetent. And that's perfectly natural. Dentists like to keep their issues close to the vest. But, Carl, you called. That's a big step — to admit that you can't figure this out alone. That's why I spoke to you on the River Walk. I can help you, if you're willing to talk straight with me. Are you willing to do that?"

Carl knew he had a major decision to make. He could tell Sidney that he only had some minor problems with his practice. Then he could guide the conversation to a polite ending. Or, he could really share what was going on. But if he opened up and told the whole truth, that would put him at risk. The risk of being seen as unable to solve his own problems, of not being in charge, of being a failure. He was weighing the risks when Sidney spoke again.

"Look, Carl, I'm here to help. If you don't want to tell me what's going on, you don't have to, but then I can't help. However, if you're willing to open up, you'll take the first real step in getting your situation handled. You can be right or you can be happy. You decide."

"What?" asked Carl. "What do you mean I can be right or I can be happy?"

"It boils down to this, Carl. You can go on believing you

can solve these problems on your own, doing things the same way that you've always done them. In that case you'd get to be right. Right that you didn't need anyone's help. Right that the way you've always done things will see you through this rough economic patch. You get to be right, but will that make you happy? Will that really solve the problems you're facing now?"

"Why can't I be right and happy?" Carl responded.

Sidney paused. "It's a bit more complex than a phone conversation can deal with. That's why I want to know if you're willing to really tell me what's going on. Revealing the truth about your situation allows you to shift the power these thoughts have over you. When you speak your unspoken thoughts, you have them, they don't have you."

Carl considered Sidney's words. His thoughts lately had overpowered him. He'd been gripped by constant worry and was having trouble sleeping. He was on edge, jumpy. His intuition told him Sidney was right. It would feel good to unburden himself, confide his worst fears. He'd been under so much pressure. It would be like opening the floodgates.

The only question that remained for Carl was if it would make any difference.

FIVE

The Teacher Appears

"OKAY, SIDNEY." CARL HELD THE PHONE in his lap for a moment and took a deep breath. He really didn't know why it was such a hard thing for him to confide his problems to someone else, but he had decided that if Sidney wanted the truth, he'd give it to him, starting with his state of mind.

"Sidney, I have to say I'm a little nervous telling you what I'm so worried about. I just don't usually tell people my problems."

"Any idea why that's hard for you?" Sidney asked.

"I've never felt comfortable with it. Maybe it's because I think I'll look ridiculous. I'm not much of a risk taker these days."

"You and most dentists, Carl."

"Right now it's hard because I don't really know you. I'm afraid you might just write me off as someone who easily folds under a little pressure."

"Well, don't worry about what I think," Sidney reassured

him. "I need to hear your thoughts out loud. I have to understand how you see your situation. Because how you see it determines what kinds of actions you'll need to take."

The statement puzzled Carl. "Explain what you mean by that. My practice is in real trouble. Anyone who looks at it would see that. It doesn't depend on how I see it."

"Did you play any sports in high school or college, Carl?"

"What's that got to do with this?"

"I think you'll see the connection. Did you play any sports?"

"Sure, basketball in high school. I played varsity my junior and senior years."

After a slight pause, Sidney asked, "Were there times when your shot was really on, when you felt you couldn't miss?"

"Sure," answered Carl.

"What was different about those times when your shooting was hot? Or when your shot was cold? How'd that feel?"

Carl found himself frowning into the mouthpiece of the phone. "I'm not sure I understand the question. Are you asking what made the difference when I made most my shots one day and struggled another day? Is that what you're asking?"

"Yes, that's my question," Sidney said.

Carl tried to think of the 'right' answer but couldn't come up with one. He couldn't see where Sidney was going with this. "I really don't know. I just saw the basket and I shot the ball. When I was hot, I couldn't miss."

"So there were times when you couldn't miss. What was different when your shot was on?" Sidney prodded.

Carl thought about the time his team had played Crater High and he'd been on fire. He scored 28 points that game. Images of that night flooded his mind. The crowd, the noise, but most of all he had a memory of the hoop — how big the basket looked that night. He remembered thinking that he could shoot a beach ball through that orange rim every time. And that's what he told Sidney. "When I was hot the basket looked huge!"

"Exactly! The way you saw the basket determined how you shot the ball. Your perception determined your actions. The hoop looked unmissable and so you attacked it. You couldn't pass up that opportunity."

"Okay," Carl admitted, "I understand that example."

"Well," Sidney continued, "How do you see you current circumstances?"

Remembering his promise to tell it straight, Carl thought about the question for a moment and answered with his deepest fear.

"I see my situation as hopeless. I feel like I can't do anything to change it. My entire world is in chaos. I'm frustrated and dejected. And, even more worrisome, I feel like I'm becoming resigned to impending doom. I'm pretty much paralyzed by the feeling that I won't be able to turn it around and my practice will go down the tube." Carl hesitated and then, because he said he'd tell the whole truth, he admitted, "And, I'm terrified that losing my practice would mean destroying my family, too."

Sidney made no immediate response. Carl regretted his last admission. Sidney was there to help him with his business, not be his family counselor.

"That took some courage, Carl. You just got out of the stands and stepped onto the court. I think you're ready to play now because you're willing to share what's really at stake here."

"I'm not saying my family is dysfunctional or that they'll abandon me at the first sign of trouble. I just don't want them to have to deal with this. They've got their own worries," Carl explained.

Sidney was methodically measured in his response. "Now that you're on the court, now that you're committed to playing, Carl, how does the basket look?"

Sidney's basketball analogy finally clicked. Carl saw his method. "I get it, Sidney. You must have coached at one time. My dental practice is the hoop, and I'm seeing it as tiny. Nothing will go in. I'm seeing my situation in a way that leaves me feeling unable to do anything about it. Perhaps if I could see things differently, I would act differently. And I could see more clearly how to work my way out of this mess I'm in."

"Bingo," Sidney chimed in. "Change your perception, change your actions."

Carl realized he was onto something. But, even though he felt a spark of hope, he wasn't sure how to proceed. "Sidney, how do I change my perception about the situation? Right now I can hardly pay my bills, new patients aren't coming in and recall is in the tank. Everything is going downhill fast. The hoop still looks too small. How do I make the basket look big again?"

"If there was an easy answer to that, you wouldn't need my help. This isn't something we can solve tonight. It's a process and it takes time. It takes coaching."

Sidney paused and Carl immediately thought, *Okay, here comes the pitch. I can't afford my rent. Staff payroll is killing me. And now this guy has got goods to sell. He probably makes a living going to ADA conventions looking for depressed dentists.*

"Are you willing to try, Carl?"

"Try what?"

"Enlarge the hoop. See what's really possible for your practice."

Carl stayed honest and answered bluntly, "What's it going to cost me?"

Sidney laughed. "Just the way you look at everything. How's that? I'm not selling more-of-the-same advice, and I don't charge like any consultant you've ever used before."

"So, what are you asking me to commit to?"

"A weekend session at my ranch in Taos. It's a working horse ranch, but I also hold seminars and client coaching sessions there. It's a beautiful place to start seeing your world differently."

Carl wasn't sure what to think. What was Sidney's angle? What was going to be the real cost? And, if he went to Taos, he'd have to tell Veronica why he was going. He'd have to tell her the truth. Carl stalled.

"Sounds interesting, but I'm not sure I can take more

time off. I'm not even sure I have enough money to make the trip."

"Don't make that an excuse," Sidney said. "That's the really unusual part of my fee structure. I don't charge anything for the initial session, and any fees after that are linked to mutually agreed upon results. You can come on a weekend so you don't lose production time. It's a no cost hook."

Carl was perplexed. "That doesn't sound like a very viable model for a consultant. We just met this afternoon. Why are you being so generous? You don't even know me."

Sidney chuckled. "It's easy to be skeptical these days, so let me tell you a little tale you might have heard before. 'There once was a young man walking along a beach. The sun was shining and it was a beautiful day. Just down the beach, he could see an older person going back and forth between the surf's edge and the beach. The older man was picking up starfish and throwing them back into the water. Back and forth he went. As the young man approached, he could see that there were hundreds of starfish stranded on the sand as a result of a high tide.'

'The young man was struck by the apparent futility of the task. There were far too many starfish. Many of them were sure to perish. As he approached, the older man continued picking up starfish one by one and throwing them into the surf. The young man said, 'You must be crazy. There are too many starfish. You can't possibly make a difference.'

'The older man stooped down, picked up one more

starfish and threw it back into the ocean. He turned to the young man and said, 'It sure makes a difference for that one!"

Carl laughed lightly at the story. "So, I'm your starfish for the day?"

"In a manner of speaking," Sidney said. "Now, I've got a few things to do because I have an early flight tomorrow. On my business card, you have my e-mail and my website. Go check it out. Ask around. Once you're sure I'm not some kind of kook, or conman who'll fleece you, get in touch. We'll get you down to Taos, so you can get back on your game."

"Okay, that sounds reasonable. I appreciate the offer. Thanks," said Carl. Then he asked the one question that had really been nagging him since he'd first met Sidney, "Why'd you stop and talk to me this afternoon? Did I really look that desperate?"

"No, Carl, you looked *ready*."

"Ready?"

"Carl, as you get to know me, you'll find I'm fond of old adages. When I saw you, a particular saying sprang to mind."

"What was it, Sidney?"

"When the disciple is ready, the teacher appears."

SIX

The Chicken or the Truth

THE CAB FROM THE AIRPORT pulled into Carl's driveway a bit after 8 PM. He paid the driver, thinking to himself he had to find a cheaper way to get to and from the airport. He really hated to be this fixated on money.

"Receipt?" asked the driver.

"Yes," said Carl. Now, more than ever, he had to be careful to document his business expenses.

Carl tried to stay focused on how he was going to tell Veronica what had been happening with the practice. He'd taken a big step by confiding in Sidney, but he was still apprehensive. All during the plane trip home and the cab ride, he had been going over and over how he would explain to Veronica that the practice was in free fall, that he was failing as a provider for their family. He wasn't sure how his wife would take it.

Walking up to the front door along the well groomed

boxwoods and staring out across the wide, trim lawn, he thought about their lifestyle and what it would be like to lose this home. Five bedrooms, three and half baths, a gourmet kitchen with two dishwashers, a six burner Wolf gas stove. It was Veronica's dream kitchen. She loved to entertain. She loved their house.

And Jonathon and Amy? What would losing this home mean in their lives, if they had to move? Different schools. Different friends. Would they be able to adjust? Would they blame him? His stomach tightened as he turned the key in the front door.

"Hey, handsome!" Veronica shouted from upstairs, after hearing the door shut. "Glad you're home. The kids are doing their homework."

And probably texting while listening to music, thought Carl. He didn't get how the kids could do all these things at once and still learn. But what could he say, when both kids had stellar grades? More than ever he didn't want to disrupt their lives with his business problems, with his inability to cope.

"You hungry?" Veronica called down the stairs.

"Sure, I could eat." Carl hadn't eaten on the plane. He'd been preoccupied with what he would say to Veronica.

"There's some barbecue chicken in the fridge. I'll be right down."

Carl headed for the kitchen, opened the fridge and found the leftovers. *Chicken.* That seemed fitting. He'd been a chicken all these months, unable to tell Veronica what was going on. In his own mind, he had rationalized it as a way not to worry her, that somehow she couldn't handle it. That she couldn't take it — that she wouldn't take *him* — anymore.

His conversation with Sidney suddenly came back to him: *How you see it determines what actions you will take.* Not only had Carl been seeing his practice like a tiny, unhittable hoop on the basketball court, he'd been seeing his wife the same way. He'd seen Veronica as unable to handle their financial difficulties, unwilling to help him out of this jam. It was *his* perception that was making their marriage fragile. He really didn't know what she thought. He hadn't asked. He had chickened out.

Veronica appeared in the kitchen entrance. "Boy, am I glad you're home." She gave him a kiss on the cheek. "And not just because I missed you. Jonathon could really use some chemistry help tonight. He's got a unit test tomorrow."

"Glad to know I'm still needed around here."

"Always."

"Really?" Carl had intended his retort to sound lighthearted, but it came out as a dark, almost despairing challenge.

Veronica looked intently at her husband, looking for some meaning in his slightly off-kilter tone. Carl turned away.

"Carl, what's wrong? Did something happen in San Antonio?"

Still holding the container of leftover chicken in his hands, Carl knew he could get out of this by avoiding the truth. He could say he was just tired, that he hadn't slept well during the conference. He could smooth this over, like barbecue sauce on chicken. But where would that leave him? With leftovers. A leftover dental practice. A leftover marriage.

He turned back and met his wife's worried gaze. "Veronica, we need to talk."

"That's obvious, Sherlock," she said, and managed to crack half a smile.

That half smile was all the opening Carl needed. It allowed him to see her again as his partner, not just some beneficiary of his paycheck. She'd helped him build his practice. She wasn't some sparrow who'd fly off at the first scent of trouble. Carl couldn't believe he'd been so tunnel-visioned.

He tossed the chicken onto the counter, stepped across the kitchen and took Veronica's hand. "Sorry. I've avoided telling you for months, but I didn't know how," said Carl.

And there, in their gourmet kitchen, he told Veronica the whole truth about how the practice had lost all its momentum, about the loss of revenue, about the dramatic drop in new patients, about their pending financial problems unless something changed.

Veronica listened. When Carl had finished with another apology for waiting so long to tell her, she squeezed his hand firmly and looked him hard in the eye.

"I can understand why you didn't tell me, and on some level I appreciate that, but I'm still mad. Not mad because things have gone south in the practice. The whole economy is teetering. I'm irritated because, well, we're a team. And you don't sell your partner short. We've gotten though a lot together. We'll get through this, but it's not something either of us will do alone."

Carl felt so ashamed he wanted to turn away, but Veronica wouldn't let him. "Okay," she said, "now that I've vented my wrathful indignation, I'm over the fact that you wanted to play Superman and fix the world economy by yourself."

"That's it? I'm not in the doghouse for weeks?"

"Look, we've got a dental practice to revive. I need you around here, not off sulking in some doghouse. So, did you come back from San Antonio with a plan of action or what?"

Carl realized what a total fool he'd been. For the first time in months he felt lucky. He told Veronica about Sidney, about their meeting, about his offer and why he thought he should make the trip to Taos.

Veronica agreed. "Carl, I've always trusted you to do what you think is best and, other than leaving me out of the loop the last few months, you've been solid. So, if you think going to New Mexico is what you need, go for it. I'm going to start working out how we can tighten our belts here at home."

Carl embraced Veronica. "You're amazing. How'd I get so lucky?"

"No mystery there," Veronica said. "It's simply a case of love."

"Thanks, for being here for me."

"Always."

They kissed.

After a blissful few moments, Carl said, "I'll go say 'Hi' to the kids and see if Jonathon needs any help with his chemistry."

"Finish your dinner first, honey. You must be starved."

Carl looked over at the leftovers on the counter. It didn't appeal to him anymore. He'd had enough *chicken* for a while.

SEVEN

Road to the Ranch

A FEW WEEKS LATER CARL STOOD in the Albuquerque airport. As he exited the baggage claim area in search of rental car desks, he saw a tall Native American with long braided hair, dressed in a dark blue work shirt and faded jeans standing among the limo drivers. He was holding a sign with the name: Dr. Carl Oldquist.

Though surprised, Carl approached him and introduced himself, "I'm Carl Oldquist."

The man nodded. "I'm Richard. I manage Sidney's ranch. I was in town picking up supplies and the boss asked me to pick you up. You got any other luggage?"

"No." Carl was traveling light with one carry-on bag and his laptop.

Richard nodded and headed for the parking lot. Carl hustled to catch up. The temperature was in the mid-80s and the warmth felt good after the chill of the plane's air conditioning. Richard led the way to short term parking and stopped next to a dirt-caked F-150 that must have been

10-12 years old. Richard put Carl's carry-on bag in the bed of the truck.

As filthy as the outside of the truck was, the inside was spotless. Not in a new or restored way, just clean. Richard started the engine and pulled out into the bright sunshine. Richard didn't say a word as they drove north toward Santa Fe on I-25. Carl tried to make small talk, but Richard didn't volunteer much in the way of detail. That he was the foreman on Sidney's ranch and had been working there close to twenty years was all that Carl could get out of him.

As they approached Santa Fe, Richard asked Carl if he needed a rest stop. Carl shook his head and Richard continued through town. As they merged onto Highway 68 traveling north, the sign read: Taos 71 miles.

Riding in an old truck with the taciturn Native American, the two and a half hours passed more quickly than Carl would have guessed. Having never been to the Southwest, he was impressed by the majesty of the distant mountains and the austerity of the sage brush, scrub oak, twilight juniper and cacti. But his attention alternated between the amazing scenery and what he hoped Sidney would be able to do for his business.

Passing vast stretches of wire and wood fences, with high desert all around, Richard finally turned off onto a side road. He stopped in front of a large 20-foot wooden arch with a seven-foot tall black metal gate. Carved deeply into the wooden arch was *Values Ranch & Retreat Center*.

Reading the sign, Carl again had his doubts. *What am I doing here? Am I out of my mind? Am I really that hopeless* that I had to come to a place in the middle of nowhere for answers? Maybe Veronica shouldn't be trusting my judgment after all.

Richard cranked his dusty window open and pressed a code into the keypad on the raised black box outside the gate. The gate opened slowly and Richard drove another half mile, finally stopping in front of a large, three-story adobe building. The entry had massive doors. Over the entry something was engraved. From the truck, Carl squinted his eyes and read: *Many victories require that you first surrender.*

Without saying a word, Richard got out of the truck and grabbed Carl's luggage. Carl repacked his laptop and was about to get out when Richard opened his door for him.

He stared directly into Carl's eyes. "Good luck, Carl. Taos can teach you a lot. Just keep your eyes open."

"Why?" asked Carl. "Is it dangerous? Are there snakes?"

"Of course," Richard smiled, "but that's not what you need to be afraid of."

Richard stepped away from the door and Carl got out. "What do you mean?"

Richard pointed to the saying above the entrance. "You've come a long way for help. You think you've arrived, but your journey is just starting. Surrender to it." Richard turned and started towards the main doors.

This journey's getting stranger all the time, Carl thought. He was taken off guard by Richard's comments. He reread the saying over the main doors and wondered what it meant. *How could you win by surrendering?*

A chill went through him, as much from the engraved words as from the drop in temperature. This was the high desert and it was approaching evening. Thirty or forty degree daily temperature swings were the norm. As he closed the pickup door and turned to follow Richard, two huge black labs came galloping up, sniffing him and barking.

The main doors of the entrance were now open and there stood Sidney. He wore Jensen boots, a cowboy hat, a pearl button blue work-shirt, jeans, and a three inch plain tan belt with a large metal buckle that had the word VALUOCITY engraved on it. No more Colonel Sanders in a white suit. He looked like a rancher that meant business.

"Welcome to Taos, Carl. Come on in," said Sidney.

Carl walked up the steps feeling as out of place as if he'd walked into a women's bathroom by mistake. *Yes*, he thought, *I'm not in Kansas anymore. Better keep my eyes out for the yellow brick road. And any wicked witches.* He crossed the threshold and shook Sidney's hand vigorously, feeling both gratitude and uncertainty.

EIGHT

Fierce Eagle and Failing Mouse

THE ENTRANCE OPENED UP INTO a Great Room two stories tall. The interior was also adobe with a large fireplace set in river rock dominating the back wall. Two long leather sofas were set perpendicular to the fireplace with three enormous leather chairs at the far end, creating a horseshoe effect opening to a crackling fire. The floors were wide oak planks. To the left, built in book shelves rose eight feet high, covering the entire length of the room. They were filled top to bottom with books, framed photos and awards.

"This is impressive, Sidney," Carl said.

"Well, it's home — and a lot more. It's your home for the next two days. We're pretty informal around here, but we mean business." He smiled and nodded at Richard who was standing behind them. "I'm sure Fierce Eagle gave you an overview of the ranch on your drive in?"

Fierce Eagle? Carl realized that must be Richard's Indian name. He wondered what his own Indian name would be. Probably something like *Failing Mouse,* he thought.

"Richard gave me some advice," Carl admitted.

"I'm sure he did. He likes results." Sidney smiled knowingly at Richard. "Now, I bet you'd like to get settled in your room. We can meet back here in, say, twenty minutes and have a snack and a drink and get started. We won't have dinner until seven.

"Fierce Eagle, please show Carl to Room 4 in the guest wing," Sidney instructed.

Richard led the way up the broad wooden staircase to the right of the fireplace, and Carl followed. At the top of the staircase a large window opened out onto forever. There wasn't another building in sight. Turning right down a long hallway, Richard opened the second door on the left and motioned Carl in. "Hope you like it," he said.

The room had textured walls, a small fireplace, and a king sized bed with a Navajo pattern quilt. Colorful lithographs adorned the walls and French doors lead out to a balcony with a stunning view of the mountains.

Carl was genuine in his reply, "This is spectacular!" He set his laptop case down on the bed. "Oh, thanks for picking me up, Rich…" Carl hesitated. "Sorry, do you prefer to be called Richard or Fierce Eagle?"

"However, you see me, Carl." And with that Richard, Fierce Eagle, let out the briefest of chuckles, slapped Carl on the back and left the way he'd come.

Carl, the Failing Mouse, stood there shaking his head, his shoulder stinging slightly. Everything was sounding so mysterious, like a puzzle he couldn't quite wrap his brain around. He sat down on the bed, looked out the French doors at the wide expanse of scrub brush, rock, sand and the biggest sky he'd ever seen hanging above the distant mountains. The vast expanse made him feel very small and all alone.

Then a single thought brightened his mood: Veronica. Quick as a whistle, he flipped his phone open and was calling home. That was one puzzle he'd already put back together, thanks in part to Sidney. He didn't have to do things alone.

When she answered the phone and he started to tell her about Richard the Fierce Eagle and Carl the Failing Mouse, he knew he could get through anything Taos had to throw his way. He knew because he wasn't doing this for himself; it was for Veronica and his family.

NINE

The Payoff

THERE WERE NO OTHER PEOPLE in the Great Room when Carl made his way back downstairs. The fire blazed and its warmth relaxed him. He walked around the room admiring the Navaho rugs, ceremonial masks and Native American paintings that gave the room its unique character. He was perusing the bookshelves when Sidney emerged from the kitchen wheeling a cart with coffee and tea as well as an assortment of sweet snacks.

"Here you go, Carl, something to hold you until dinner."

"Coffee is just what I need, thanks," Carl said appreciatively. He went to the service cart and picked up the mug Sidney had poured for him. Sidney poured himself a cup and took a seat on the leather sofa closest to the fireplace.

"Have a seat. How was your flight?"

Carl sat opposite Sidney. "It wasn't too bad. Went by fast."

"And your family is doing well?"

"Yes, in fact, I called my wife from the room." Carl hung his head. "She knows. Our talk in San Antonio shamed me into talking to her. She's really on my side. I'd forgotten that, I guess."

"I'm glad to hear you're opening up," said Sidney. "Okay. Are you ready to get started?"

Carl nodded. The crackle of the fire seemed louder now. Was it because he was entering new territory and his alertness was heightened?

"Alright, Carl, tell me how your practice is showing up for you these days?"

"What do you mean by 'showing up?'"

"Don't worry. I use a lot of jargon, so some of the questions I'll ask over the next couple days might not make sense to you at first. Tell me when you don't understand something. There might be questions you've never asked yourself before or concepts you may be unfamiliar with. Some of my questions will require you to look at yourself — not your circumstances. Are you following?"

Carl took a quick sip from his mug. "Not entirely."

"In order for you to dig yourself and your practice out of the hole you're in, you have to stop trying to change the circumstances and start changing yourself," Sidney explained.

Carl felt his heart beat a little faster; he was beginning to feel a little nervous. "What do I have to change?"

"Remember when we talked on the phone in San Antonio and you described some of your high school basketball experiences. You said you had games where you couldn't miss. During those games, you said the basket was huge. That's what I mean by showing up. How does your practice show up for you, how does it occur for you now, in the middle of this recession, in the midst of the shrinking results you are producing?"

Carl now understood the question. Sidney wanted to know how he perceived his practice in its current condition. How was he feeling about his practice now? That was easy to do.

He spilled his guts. All the bad numbers. All the paralyzing indecision. All the remorse for not trusting Veronica. All the worry about how this could affect his family. All the shame at not being able to pull his practice out of the downward spiral.

After he was finished, Sidney didn't speak for a moment. He sipped his coffee, and then said, "The question was, 'How is your practice showing up for you?' What I heard, and correct me if I'm wrong, is your practice is falling down the rabbit hole. You see yourself as incapable of taking effective action and you are doomed to failure. Is that what you said?"

"Yes," Carl said, unable to look Sidney in the eye. He felt he'd said too much and had really exposed himself. He was embarrassed. He'd blown his façade of confidence and now he really did feel like *Failing Mouse*.

"I understand how you could see it that way, Carl. I appreciate how much you care about your practice, your profession and your family. And I understand why you feel unable to turn it around." Sidney paused to check his watch.

"Before dinner I have a homework assignment for you to complete. It's critical that you do your homework and take it seriously. Will you do it?"

"That's why I came," Carl answered.

"Here's your assignment. I want you to examine your internal dialogue, that little voice inside your head telling you that your situation is hopeless. This is only an interpretation of reality. It is not the truth. It is made-up. This is the way you see it and isn't necessarily accurate. Once you've written down your internal dialogue, I want you to list what it costs you to hold onto these interpretations of helplessness. Then I want you to list the payoffs to keep these interpretations going. Carl, would you please repeat back to me what you heard me ask you to do."

"You want me to consider the little voice in my head that is evaluating and judging me, which has concluded I am unable to reverse my practice's downward drift. You asked me to look at why I am holding onto this interpretation and write down what it costs me to do so, and what is the payoff for holding on to this interpretation. Although, I can't, honestly, imagine any payoff in all this mess."

"Believe me, there is a big payoff in it for you," said Sidney. "Looks like you're clear on the assignment. It's about six. Be down here for dinner at seven. Okay?"

Sidney stood up as did Carl. "Thanks, Sidney."

"Don't thank me yet. We've just started. Do your homework."

Sidney turned and wheeled the beverage cart back towards the kitchen.

I'm not seeing much of any payoff in any of this, Carl thought as he headed back up the stairs to his room.

TEN

Homework Aha

ONCE BACK IN HIS ROOM, Carl decided a shower might help him think; he certainly needed one after the long day of travel. He grabbed his travel kit and went into the bathroom. Everything was top notch: granite counters, pewter fixtures, stone floor, marble shower, luxurious towels.

He took a long hot shower. The shower head was large and the pressure was strong. It relaxed him as he mentally worked through the homework Sidney had given him. He still could not see any payoff that his current view of the situation was providing, but he certainly knew the costs.

Once out of the shower and dried off, Carl dressed in jeans and a white t-shirt under a V-neck hunter green sweater. He figured this would be appropriate dress for dinner on the ranch. He got out his computer and was pleased to discover the ranch had Wi-Fi. He first checked his e-mail to see if there was anything urgent. Nothing but a few e-mails from his front desk and two from colleagues.

He responded to the e-mails and then opened a Word document to start on his homework.

The internal dialogue was easy. He'd been living with that little voice telling him that things were going to hell in a handbasket for months. That voice had told him whatever he did wouldn't make any difference. No matter what, he'd be labeled a loser if he couldn't right the practice himself. That little voice had been an insufferable companion during the downturn.

He finished the internal dialogue quickly. Then he typed the word 'Costs.' He'd been worrying about the decline of his practice for months, so the costs flew off his fingertips and onto the screen. His immediate income. His future financial security. His staff's jobs. His practice's viability. His relationships with his wife and kids. Their future together. It cost him a sense of well being. And it cost him his self esteem.

Not a happy list at all. Just writing it down made Carl wonder how he could find anything to put under the heading 'Payoff' which he dutifully, though skeptically, typed. He stared at the word, for a very long time. Nothing came to mind, absolutely nothing.

He got up from his chair and went to the French doors, looking out into the endless sky that was deepening to indigo. Off in the distance he spotted the silhouette of a large bird gliding effortlessly on the cool evening breeze.

What was it Richard had told him when they first arrived at the ranch? Something about surrendering to the journey. It was even engraved above the main doors: *Many victories require that you first surrender.*

What was Carl supposed to surrender to? Was that part of the 'payoff' of this homework? He asked himself again, *What's my payoff? What do I get out of feeling unable? What's my reward for feeling powerless?*

He watched the large bird circling in the distance. *Maybe an eagle hunting some hapless victim,* Carl mused with a grim smile. Then, suddenly, the bird's wide wings swept back and it dove to the ground like a lightning bolt. Carl was electrified. *Some poor 'failing mouse' just bit it,* he reasoned. *Sucks to be him.*

Just as suddenly as the bird of prey's strike, Carl was struck with the 'payoff.' He hurried to his computer. His fingers hurrying over the keyboard like a mouse seeking safety.

ELEVEN

The Challenge

LONG BEFORE HE REACHED THE BOTTOM of the stairs, Carl drifted into the savory smell coming from the kitchen. Sidney was sitting in one of the leather arm chairs facing the fire.

"You look refreshed and a little brighter," Sidney commented casually. "I must not have given you tough enough homework."

"It was tough, but it taught me something."

"Good, we'll get to it right after dinner. I'm starved. Richard's wife, Dawn, cooked for us tonight. When we have a larger group, she supervises the meals, but tonight she cooked it all, a traditional Pueblo dish, elk stew and corn." Sidney stood and motioned Carl to follow him.

The kitchen was expansive. Pots and pans hung from a wrought iron oval rack over a large, well used gas range. Tall cabinets of pine hung above turquoise-tiled counters. The far corner of the kitchen had a built-in nook with a bay window that seemed to float over the ghostly desert lit with the ranch's floodlights. The table was set for four. Sidney went and sat down. "We'll eat here for most of our meals. You're our only guest this weekend, so we're keeping it informal."

Richard and Dawn suddenly appeared through a side door. Whereas Richard was tall and rugged, all sharp angles and no nonsense, Dawn was short and softly rounded in a flannel shirt and broad denim skirt that swept around her ankles when she walked. Her hair was pulled back revealing a calm and benevolent face.

"Welcome to Taos," she said to Carl. "Welcome to the ranch."

"Thank you," said Carl. "Dinner smells great."

Dawn smiled demurely and brought over a small pitcher. She poured into the four glasses a thin, cream-colored liquid. Carl looked puzzled, until Sidney explained, "Dawn has prepared a drink made of corn which is really quite a treat. We'll use it to toast your visit and that your work here will speed your transformation." He held up his glass to Carl's.

"My transformation?" Carl cast a suspicious eye towards Richard who was bringing a steaming pot to the table.

"The changes *you'll* need to make to solve your problems," Sidney answered. "But let's not talk shop while we eat. Let's try some good old fashioned southwestern small talk."

Surprisingly, Carl found it easy to just chat with these almost complete strangers. Sidney was a master at getting people to talk about themselves. He had Carl going on about his family and what it was like to live in Madison.

Then Sidney got Dawn to talk about her own children. It was good for Carl to see Richard's serious face turn a bit lighter as Dawn talked about their son working for the US Forest Service and their daughter who was in the nursing program at Arizona State University.

So, Carl thought, *even Mr. Fierce Eagle has a softer side.* He wondered how he should really try to 'see' this enigmatic Native American who had told him to surrender.

After eating, Carl didn't have to embellish his compliments on the tastiness of the elk stew. His three generous helpings spoke for themselves. They all helped bus the table and then Dawn shooed Carl and Sidney out of the kitchen. "You've got your business to do. Leave us with ours."

Sidney led Carl back into the Great Room and they took their seats by the fire. "Alright, Carl, let's see how you did on your homework. What are the costs and payoffs of your current mindset?"

"Let me go get my laptop and I'll show you."

He stood to go get the computer from his room, but Sidney stopped him. "I don't want you to read your answers to me. I want you to speak them."

"But, I might miss something," said Carl.

"Don't worry. You'll remember what you need to remember."

Carl sat back down and considered what he had written. "Okay. The costs were easy. Seeing myself as incapable of handling the downturn in my practice has cost me financially. Other costs are my relationships, the future of my business, and certainly my peace of mind — and a whole hell of a lot of sleep."

"Indeed," said Sidney. "Excellent. Okay, you said the costs were easy. What about the payoffs?"

"At first, I couldn't think of anything. What payoffs could I possibly get from holding myself as a failure, as totally incapable? And then it hit me. If I'm incapable, I won't take any action since I know it's bound to fail. So, one payoff is that I don't have to take any chances, or risk anything. And if I don't do anything, I can't fail."

Sidney nodded in approval.

Carl went on with confidence. "I also considered that I don't have to change. I can just be the way I've always been because it worked in the past. I don't have to take any chances. So again, it's a way of reducing my risk."

"How does that reduce your risk?" Sidney asked.

"Well, I can make others responsible. I can blame Bush and Obama for what happened to the economy. I can blame my current situation on my location, my staff, my office manager, the people I pay to advertise, patients not having money, and so on. That's the real payoff. I get to blame everyone else. I'm the innocent victim. I'm just in the wrong place at the wrong time — like a mouse becoming an eagle's dinner."

"An important insight," Sidney said. "Blame and fault are the antithesis of responsibility. That's what most dentists are doing now. Blaming everything and everyone for their situation. Not taking responsibility. No responsibility, no power."

"I'm beginning to see that," said Carl. "And the more I blame others for my problems, the more stuck I become."

"Exactly!" exclaimed Sidney, his eyes lighting up.

"And another thing, and this isn't on my computer upstairs, I get to make people wrong."

"Tell me more about that, Carl."

"I can blame lots of people for my situation. My staff, because they're not getting the job done. My wife, because she should somehow see what's going on without me telling her. My kids, because they should care about me and know how hard I work. And, I know this sounds strange," Carl hung his head slightly as he said it, somewhat ashamed, "but I can even blame my Dad because he somewhat pushed me into dentistry."

Sidney nodded sympathetically. "No, that doesn't sound strange at all. When people feel they are losing, the natural tendency is to blame others and make them wrong. It's just one way of avoiding responsibility for the situation. And, as I said, if there's no responsibility, there's no power. You've made some good progress here."

"Thanks. What's next?" Carl asked.

"Hold on just a minute. Let's review your payoffs again and see if I understood what you said. The payoffs you get from holding yourself as incapable are 1) you get to decrease your risks, 2) you get to blame and fault others, and 3) you get to make others wrong, which allows you not to be responsible. Is that a fair summation?"

"Definitely," Carl said.

"There's one more payoff that you're right on the edge of seeing. And that is when you blame others, when you make it their fault, when you make them wrong, in essence you make yourself right. And that is the biggest payoff of all. You get to be right!"

"I get to be *right*?"

"Yes," said Sidney. "Remember when we talked on the phone in San Antonio, I told you that most people would rather be right than happy."

"I don't think I understand it in relation to my current situation. I think I'd love to be wrong about the fact that my practice is about to crash and burn."

Sidney looked Carl in the eyes. "When we've talked, you made everything and everyone wrong about your situation. When we talked about the practice, you made your practice wrong for not taking care of you. You made your staff wrong for not caring enough. You made your wife and your kids wrong. You made the ADA and third parties wrong. And worst of all, you made yourself wrong."

"How'd I make myself wrong if I was trying to make myself right?"

"Don't you see, by making others wrong, you made yourself right about not being good enough or smart enough to figure this out. You made yourself all wrong to fit your perception that you could do nothing about your situation. This is what you need to transform."

Carl broke in. "That's what you toasted before dinner: my transformation. What does that mean?"

"In my work, it means operating beyond your history, beyond your past, beyond your personality and beyond your psychology," Sidney explained.

"Well, what is there beyond your past, your personality and psychology?" asked Carl.

"You'll find out," replied Sidney. "Let's say for now that your history, your personality and even your psychology are all past-based. Therefore, your future is pretty much guaranteed to turn out just like your past. For your situation to change, you have to change. That's what these next two days are about."

Carl's head was swirling. Transformation, beyond his past, beyond his personality. This didn't sound too practical and Carl liked to think of himself as a practical guy. "I'm not sure what you're asking me to do here."

Sidney leaned forward in his seat. "Tonight you need to decide if you'd rather be right or happy. If you decide to give up blaming others, making others wrong, making others responsible, if you are willing to give up being right, then we can get some work done. If not, the rest of our weekend will be a waste of time."

Sidney stood up and put his hands in his pockets. "It's a lot to lay on you, Carl, but it's vital to how I coach. I'm more of a coach than a consultant. I think you can appreciate that from your basketball days. I've given you a personal challenge, so think it over and let me know what you've decided at breakfast tomorrow. There's an alarm in your room. Breakfast is at 7:00 sharp in the kitchen. Sleep well."

Carl turned and stared at the fireplace as Sidney left the room. Sidney's challenge was clear. The problem was, as Carl watched the waning flames of the fire, he wasn't really sure he was up to the challenge.

Once back in his room, Carl set his alarm for 6:15. But lying in bed, he was unable to sleep. Sidney's challenge kept echoing in his mind. Was he willing to change?

He had to make a choice. And if he chose to stay at the ranch, he'd have to give up making people wrong. He'd have to give up making himself wrong. He'd have to take responsibility. Most of his thinking, most of his conversations with his peers, conversations with nearly everybody, had been about making the economy, the government, his staff and his family wrong. Was he really willing to give that up? And if he did, what would he replace it with?

Finally, the weight of the day — the traveling, the newness, the challenges to his perceptions — pressed Carl into a fitful sleep.

TWELVE

Surrender

THE ALARM SOUNDED LOUDLY AT 6:15. The events of yesterday came back in a flash and Sidney's challenge hit him like a hammer. What really weighed on Carl was not knowing what the future was going to look like if he changed. No matter how bad things were now, at least he knew what he had. It was known, constant.

He thought about calling Veronica, but it was Saturday. After a week of getting the kids going early and keeping them on track, she deserved to sleep in. *Besides,* he thought, *it's not the practice she cares about, it's only the income it produces.*

Carl stopped himself and considered this last thought. Was that really true? Of course it wasn't. Veronica cared about the practice. She'd helped establish it. She knew the staff. Many of his patients were her friends. She was proud of the service the practice provided. With burning clarity, Carl saw how he was making her wrong just to support his negative perspective.

Would I rather be right or happy? I'm making people wrong to make my views right. *How can I make anything right if I'm always making someone wrong?*

Carl now understood why Sidney talked in terms of his transformation. The situation around him did not have to change, he had to change in order to truly tackle his problems. Could he do that?

The vivid scene he had witnessed yesterday evening of the eagle striking down its unsuspecting prey filled his mind. Did he want to be that unsuspecting victim? That Failing Mouse?

The engraving above the front doors of the ranch came back to him: *Many victories require that you first surrender.*

Surrender.

Richard had advised him to do that. But *surrender* meant *defeat* to Carl. Or was that just another thing Carl was seeing as negative? In many ways, he already felt defeated. Yet, surrender also meant to give in, to bow to the inevitable. Could he really find victory in that kind of surrender? To surrender a perspective that seemed as much a part of him as breathing? Was he really willing to make that kind of change?

The answer was obvious. He wanted to make the change; he was willing to surrender his negative perspective. The only remaining question was whether he could really do it.

Now Carl was really scared.

THIRTEEN

A Question of Excellence

"GOOD MORNING," SIDNEY CALLED OUT heartily as Carl entered the kitchen. There was a place setting and a steaming cup of black coffee waiting for Carl. "Did you sleep soundly?"

"Honestly, Sidney, not that well. You gave me a lot to think about."

"Well, have you decided?" asked Sidney. "Are you willing to move forward?"

Though his trepidation made him hesitate, Carl was clear in his response. "The answer is 'Yes.' I do want to learn more, and I know I need to let go of some of my previous thinking. I'm just hoping I can. I've realized how ingrained my habit of making others wrong is."

"I knew it wouldn't be an easy night for you," Sidney reassured him. "It's tough to surrender — even a negative aspect of your character. Letting go of making yourself and others wrong is a difficult habit to break. But I can't teach someone who isn't responsible, and when you make others and yourself wrong, it displaces responsibility."

"Well, Sidney, I realized that's all I do now. I make people wrong. I mean not just a little bit, but a lot. When I chat with my fellow colleagues, I make others wrong. When I talk to some staff individually, I make other staff wrong. I see that most of my assumptions about people and things are making them wrong. And, yes, I understand that it makes me right. Now I understand your riddle: People would rather be right than happy."

"Okay, Carl, that's fine, but don't make yourself wrong for having an insight about making people wrong. Most people are unconscious about doing it, and they do it all the time. But now that you know the payoff and not just the cost, now that you recognize what you have been doing and you can see how you operate, you can make a choice. You don't have to make people or circumstances wrong."

"I'm hoping that's what the rest of the weekend is about," Carl said.

"In essence, it is, and it starts by getting to the core. Your core."

"My core?"

"Yes indeed." Sidney chuckled lightly and took a long sip of his coffee. "Let me try to get at this by asking you a question. What do you base your practice on?"

Carl looked at Sidney curiously. "I'm not sure what you mean? Remember, it's early and I had a restless night. Can you give me a little help?"

"Sure. I mean what's the core, the nucleus, the soul of your practice? What do you base your decisions on? How do you determine who to hire and when to fire? What is it that you base your practice on?"

Carl stared into his coffee for a second before looking up a Sidney. "I never really thought about my practice that way. It seemed to be an automatic sequence. You know, college, dental school, military, a residency program, an associateship, then purchasing a practice. I took the road most dentists take, I guess. I simply thought that if I went into practice, did good dentistry, took care of my patients, hired good people, kept up with my CE, and followed the systems and structures that consultants taught me about practice management, it would just all work out."

Sidney nodded his head. "It's a story I've heard many times before, and when times are good it doesn't seem to matter that you don't really know what your practice stands on. But now, Carl, because of this economic storm, you don't know how much your practice can weather. You don't know how sturdy the foundation is — or if there is a real foundation. So, in essence, you've got nothing to stand on, nothing to support you from which to rebuild. No wonder you're feeling like your practice is falling apart."

"Well," Carl said, "I didn't anticipate an economic crisis like this. I didn't expect the dramatic drop off in new patients, revenues and case acceptance. I didn't expect to be going broke."

"Who did?" retorted Sidney flatly. "The fact is that in your current trajectory you are going broke. And whatever your practice is built on, whatever determines your foundation, doesn't work in this new economy. So, if you are going to have a practice that works, we need to start with the most critical and fundamental piece. We need to get to the core of your beliefs."

Sidney let that sink in a moment and then asked, "What is the basis for your practice? What is at its foundation?"

"Alright, I think I can answer that now," Carl responded. "My practice is built on excellence."

Sidney turned away from Carl and looked out the window. "Sorry," Sidney said, turning back to Carl, "I hear that word *excellence* far too many times when I ask this question of dentists, and it aggravates me."

"Why? Isn't excellence a good thing to base a practice on?"

"My problem is I don't think you really mean it. Like most dentists I believe you said it because you think it's the right thing to say. That it's safe. That no one can argue with the concept of excellence. But I don't think you, like most of your colleagues, have a clue as to what *excellence* really means."

Sidney's accusation upset him. Carl took hundreds of hours of CE; he studied with the top clinicians; he'd spent hundreds of thousands of dollars over the last 10 years on training, education and development to become a top of the line provider. He was *always* striving for excellence.

"Sidney, that pisses me off. Who are you to tell me my practice isn't about excellence?"

"Carl, I'm the guy who isn't going broke. I'm the

guy who's helped hundreds of dentists become and stay successful. I'm the guy who knows that for you excellence is a cliché, not a stand you take about your entire practice."

"My clinical skills are not a cliché," Carl countered emphatically.

"Besides your clinical dentistry, tell me what other aspects of your practice are excellent. Is your staff excellent? Do you have a group of people who can seize the initiative and act, rather than wait to be given instructions? I know you know how each staff member operates. You know their skill levels. You know which ones are accountable and who is there only for the paycheck. You know whether they are optimistic or pessimistic, team players or loners, givers or takers. Do you have a staff person that you can honestly say is excellent?"

Carl thought for a moment, visualizing each of his staff members. "I'm not sure I know how to make that evaluation."

"I think you do, Carl. Does any one of your staff perform consistently at championship level? Do they deliver excellence in their work and their interactions? Do they get the job done individually as well as contribute to the team with excellent performance?"

Carl thought of his hygienist, Sheila. She was a total prima-donna, not at all a team player. She never helped at the front, frequently talked down to the assistants, often arrived late for the morning meetings, or not at all.

Then he thought about Sharon, his front desk person. She was really the office manager. She ran the practice.

She'd been with him for 12 years, but she was the person most resistant to change. Every time he brought in a consultant, she quietly fought it. When he wanted to go paperless, she was like a parachute tied to a runner. When he wanted to change how patients were confirmed, she always offered the same refrain: 'Our systems work fine the way they are. Why change?'

"Well?" asked Sidney again. "Do you have even one excellent staff person?"

Carl shook his head regrettably, "No."

"How about your tracking systems, your customer service, your marketing? Are all parts of your practice striving for excellence like you are in your clinical dentistry? Or is 'good enough' good enough for you?"

It was Carl's turn to look out the kitchen window and catch his breath. "Okay, I get it, but what does this have to do with me getting out of this deep hole?" Carl responded softly when he turned back to face Sidney. "I can't go back and fire my entire staff."

"No, you don't have to fire your staff. You have to figure out if you can truly make excellence a core element of your practice or not. And if you can, you need to be committed to making it happen in every part of your practice, not just in your work on crowns, bridges and implants."

Sidney took a breath and then continued in an even tone. "You say that excellence is core for you, but when you really examine your day-to-day operations, it doesn't appear to be at the heart of your practice. You operate as if excellence is optional, not mandatory."

"Yeah, I guess that's right," Carl admitted with a sigh.

"Good. That's the first step. The next step is to identify your core values. Once you have this foundation, you'll be able to take a stand and operate consistent with that core. Make it the bedrock of your practice. And it's crucial that you build a core that isn't based on the current economic conditions. You need a core that is purely your self-expression. A core that will enable the practice to meet any challenge and overcome any circumstance."

"How do I do that?"

Sidney grabbed a folder that had been on the far corner of the table. He opened it and handed Carl a legal pad with a pen. "I want you to take an hour, go anywhere you like in the lodge or on the property, and write down your core values."

"I thought excellence was one of my core values, but you killed that one. Can you give me some ideas on how to generate this list?" Carl asked.

"Think about it this way," Sidney explained. "What is the core of your practice? You are. How is your core expressed? It's expressed as values — core values. Core values are a direct expression of who you are. Without core values clearly and solidly as the foundation of your practice, it won't be able to right itself in this economic mess.

"Carl, ask yourself: If you were a patient, what core values would you want your dentist to have? If you were a staff member, what core values would you want as the fabric of your practice culture? If you were an associate looking to purchase a practice, what core values would you seek in a practice?"

"So," Carl began, "as the owner and operator of my practice, what do I stand for? Is that what you're asking me to identify?"

"Yes," Sidney responded. "Core values are those values that are at the heart of who you are. They are those values that determine how you live your life. Core values shape your thinking and action. Core values ultimately determine your relationships. Core values are guiding principles and tenants that determine your philosophy of practice and of life. Core values are those values that you hold inviolate."

"And writing down my core values will save my practice?" Carl asked, looking a bit bewildered.

"Carl, that's where you have to start. The big challenge is to make your core values live and breathe in the practice, beyond just showing up as a list of inspirational words hanging on the wall in your office. When core values are neither honored nor upheld, the essence, the mettle of the practice is weak and shallow. Without core values being venerated, the practice doesn't have the necessary energy to effectively confront, nor take authoritative action when challenged. It is fundamental and critical for practice success that you and the staff respect and faithfully adhere to the core values. Is that clear?"

"How do I get my staff to follow the core values? That's going to be a huge change."

"You're absolutely right, but we're getting ahead of ourselves. We'll handle that once you've declared your core values and generated your core beliefs. For now just ask yourself, 'What are my core values?' This will take some self-reflection. You can't find these values outside of yourself. No consultant, advisor, book or blog can give you the answer. No one can tell you what core values to have. There are no 'right' core values!"

"Sidney, how will I know they're really core values? How can I be sure they are true core values and not just made up like *excellence*?"

Sidney reached inside the folder and handed Carl a printed form. "If your core value makes it through this gauntlet, it's legitimate. If you cannot answer 'Yes' to all of these questions it's not a true core value."

Carl read the checklist:

CORE VALUE TEST

1. If you were to start a new practice, would you build it around this core value regardless of the location or type of practice?
2. Would you want your practice to continue to stand for this core value 50 years into the future, no matter what changes occur in the outside world?
3. Would you want your practice to hold this core value, even if at some point in time it became a competitive disadvantage — even if in some instances the environment penalized the practice for living this core value?
4. Do you believe that those who do not share this core value — those who breach it consistently — simply do not belong in your practice?

5. Would you personally continue to hold this core value even if you were not rewarded for doing so?
6. Would you stop practicing before giving up this core value?
7. If you awoke tomorrow with more than enough money to retire comfortably for the rest of your life, would you continue to apply this core value to your productive activities?

"Wow, where'd you get this?" Carl exclaimed. "I don't know if anything will pass!"

"I got it from an article by Jim Collins entitled 'Vision Framework.' I adapted it to speak specifically to dentists. I can't come up with everything, you know. There are a lot of brilliant authors out there and Collins is one of them. It's on my website with everything else. You'll see."

"Okay," Carl said, not entirely convinced, "but this is gonna take some thinking."

"Alright then, get to it. We'll meet in the Great Room at 11:00, and I expect your top core values for the practice to be clearly defined."

Carl rose with the legal pad and checklist and began to walk out of the kitchen. His mind was reeling. He didn't know how he was going to come up with these.

Sidney called to him just before he passed into the Great Room, "Carl, just one more thing. Have an *excellent* time."

FOURTEEN

To the Core

JUST OUTSIDE THE KITCHEN DOOR, Carl stopped and took a breath. He was feeling somewhat overwhelmed and wasn't sure where to start. He looked around and spotted something that might help. Coffee. A pot was sitting on the counter along with some mugs. Carl went to the counter and poured himself a cup. As he poured, he noticed Sidney's credo emblazoned on the side:

> **VALUOCITY**
> YOU CAN'T FAIL
> WHEN YOU BASE
> YOUR PRACTICE
> ON YOUR VALUES

Darn him, thought Carl. *He's always one step ahead!* Though, in reality, he figured Sidney was probably more like two or three steps ahead of him. At least he understood what Sidney was asking him to do, even if he wasn't sure it would do him or his practice much good.

He headed up the stairs back to his room. Once inside, he tossed the legal pad and core values checklist on the bed. Sipping his coffee, he stood looking out the French doors. The snow-capped mountains looked larger, somewhat closer today, contrasted against a brilliant blue sky. Could beauty like that be one of his core values? Right now it seemed more important than anything else he should be doing.

Reluctantly, he glanced down at the Core Value Test. He thought, *What values do I have that would get me through this maze of indecision?* He thought about people around him he admired. His Dad. Veronica. Then, sports legends like Bill Russell, Jackie Robinson and Cal Ripken. Finally, he considered historical figures like Franklin, Jefferson, Lincoln and Roosevelt. He thought about what made them stand out and why they left such a memorable legacy. Suddenly the answer clicked.

Integrity.

That's what he wanted to be about. That's what his practice needed to be built on. Making promises and keeping them. Sticking to what was best for his patients at all times. Carl could see that as fundamental — as a core value.

On the legal pad, he wrote it down. He stared at the word. What did he need to have integrity?

Courage.

That made sense. You needed to back up your promises and stand by them and that took courage. He also wanted his practice to respect patients. He added Respect. Carl began to see what Sidney was really asking him to do here, and that helped him with the rest of his list.

He included Excellence because he did believe that was fundamental, even though Sidney had shown him he didn't fully understand what excellence looked like in all aspects of his practice. But he would have the courage to put it on his list and learn what excellence as a core value really meant.

Carl kept at it until he had his list:
1. Integrity
2. Courage
3. Respect
4. Excellence
5. Improvement
6. Service
7. $$$

He'd written the number seven down, but he struggled to find the word he was looking for. He wanted his practice to be financially successful. He wanted to have money to fund the future, to pay for new technologies and equipment. He wanted to pay the staff well. He wanted to pay himself well. He wanted to fund his retirement and the staff's retirement. But he couldn't capture the one word that expressed that value. He'd just have to ask Sidney for help on that one.

He used Sidney's checklist and put each value through the test three times. Each of the values he'd written down came through with flying colors, even ambiguous number seven. He felt ready. He looked at his watch; it was nearing eleven. He headed for the Great Room feeling a greater sense of accomplishment than he had in a long time.

FIFTEEN

Taking a Stand

AS CARL CAME DOWN THE STAIRS, he saw Sidney and Richard looking out the big windows to the left of the fireplace. Sidney was pointing to something on the grounds and giving Richard instructions. Richard was listening intently and when Sidney stopped speaking, he nodded once, turned around and walked crisply out of the room.

Sidney motioned for Carl to join him next to the hearth. Carl had his legal pad in hand.

"Well, how'd you do?" asked Sidney.

"Pretty well, I think."

"Any trouble?" Sidney inquired.

"A little. I couldn't get one value clearly articulated. I know what I want. I know what it is, but I couldn't put into a single word or phrase like the others," said Carl.

"Do you want to handle that value first or last?"

"Last, I think. I want to see if I got the others right."

"You know, Carl, there is no right or wrong when it comes to core values. They are simply an expression of who you are. What's right for you is only right for you, not anyone else. Now, tell me your core values, one at a time, and explain them to me. Tell me what they mean to you, state them as a belief or stand."

"Can you give me an example?"

"Let me see your list," Sidney said. He looked it over. "Let's take Service as an example. Service might mean something very different to you than it does to me. So, I want you tell me what each core value means to you. Is what I'm asking clear?"

Carl nodded in the affirmative. He folded back the used page of his legal pad and started fresh. "*Integrity*. I guess what I mean is that my staff and I are honest. We do what we say we will do."

"Well done. That's clear. Write that down next to the value. The more simply stated as you just did, the more powerful. Next?"

Carl jotted down his definition and continued, "*Courage*. For me, courage means having the guts to do the right thing simply because it is the right thing to do."

"Good, go on," said Sidney.

"*Respect*. Treat our patients and each other the way we would like to be treated."

Sidney nodded his approval.

"*Excellence*." Carl paused to see if Sidney would cringe or look away, as he had done at breakfast, but he remained focused, so Carl continued. "I thought about this a lot after our conversation. It is core for me. And what I mean by excellence is we strive for excellence in everything we do.

It's just not about clinical excellence. Good enough doesn't cut it anymore."

"I think you have a better grasp of excellence as a core value now. Please go on," Sidney encouraged.

"*Improvement.* To me it means we strive to get better at what we do every day."

"That value is critical to achieving excellence. It was wise of you to add that one, Carl."

"Thanks." Carl smiled. "Next, I have *Service.* I want this to mean we provide for our patients at a level higher than they have ever experienced."

Carl paused as he looked at the last value on his list. "Sidney, this is the one I'm stuck on. I don't have a name for it yet. It's about making money so we can capitalize the practice, so we can take care of our families, so we do things for our communities. It's not about making money to get rich; it's not about power or fame. It's about making money to allow us to have a vision of the practice that is achievable."

Sidney smiled. "I know exactly what you're saying. I think I know the word. It's one that most dentists don't use because they think it sounds like they are only in practice for the money. I think the word you're looking for is *Profitable.*"

"Yeah, that makes sense," Carl said as he wrote down the word. "It is absolutely core that we are profitable. Without profit, we can't take care of anyone, our patients, our practice or ourselves."

"Excellent!" Sidney grinned. "You're picking this up

quickly. Being able to express these core values as a belief or stand is essential to make them real. When you get back to your practice, you'll need to present your core values to the staff the way you just did with me," said Sidney. "Can you do that?"

His face darkening, Carl hesitated. "But, Sidney, even if I present these to the staff, I have a feeling it will be a moment of 'Wow' followed by a fairly quick return to business-as-usual. I've seen it happen too often after I've worked with consultants."

"Well, for most dental practices, that's true," Sidney explained. "In a dental practice, the core values are typically presented once and so they tend to disappear quickly. Identifying and presenting core values, without moving them into the daily operational activities, usually means they will lose power and fade into the background. But, if you declare that the core values are part of how the staff is compensated, for example, then the core values won't fade so unceremoniously."

"Can you give me a few more specifics about what that looks like?" Carl asked. "What do you mean moving the core values down to the daily operational activities and impacting the way staff gets paid?"

"When people are performing well and you acknowledge them, you also tell them how it reinforces a core value. For example, when your assistant does an outstanding job taking care of a patient, just saying 'You did a great job' is not enough. Saying 'You really showed our core value of service with Mrs. Smith' is much more specific and reinforces the core value. Or when a staff member makes a mistake or doesn't follow through, don't just talk about how that's a problem. You discuss how it does not represent or support a core value. Core values need to be the constant with which you measure your day-to-day operations. And if your evaluation of staff is tied to those core values, you can more easily document those elements for raises or bonuses as well."

Carl's face brightened and he sat up straighter. "I get it. Every day, I need to tie acknowledgment or correction to the core values. I can see doing this in our morning meetings and staff meetings. I can see it really working that way. I can see how core values would then live in the practice. But what's this about setting up staff compensation so it is connected to the core values?"

"Listen, Carl, you're right on track here. Let's stay focused, we'll get to staff evaluation tomorrow. For now you need to consider how you will know whether a staff member is embodying and fully expressing the core values in your practice."

"Do you mean how would a staff member behave if she really embraced the core values?"

"Exactly!"

"Okay. That's clearer. I need to write some of this down and sort through it," Carl said.

"You sure do." Sidney looked at his watch. "I have a conference call in about twenty minutes, so I'm going to leave you on your own for lunch. Just pop into the kitchen and tell Dawn where you'd like to eat. We'll meet back here at two. Be as specific as you can on how you'd know if you and your staff were committed to the core values every day. Good work this morning. I'll see you this afternoon."

"Thanks a ton, Sidney" Carl said, and knew he really meant it. Sidney was helping him see his practice in a new way. *Maybe*, he thought, *I should add Gratitude to my list of core values.*

SIXTEEN

No Free Lunch

DAWN KNOCKED ON THE DOOR and brought in Carl's lunch. A chicken salad sandwich, a small green salad, ice water with lemon and a delicious-smelling apple cobbler with a small carafe of strong coffee.

"Thanks, Dawn. This looks great."

"How's the work coming?" Dawn asked, eyeing the crumpled up legal pad pages on the desk and bed.

"It's coming along, but I think I have a ways to go still."

"Well, I hope it's a good journey," she said as she turned to go.

"Dawn, when I arrived at the ranch, your husband said something about surrendering to the journey."

Dawn laughed lightly and looked back over her shoulder. "He'd know about both. It was an interesting road for him to get here to the ranch. And as an Indian, he knows a lot about surrendering. Not always the right kind, though."

Then she was out the door, leaving Carl with another little mystery about Fierce Eagle. He didn't have much time to ponder it, though. His cell phone rang.

"Hey, cowboy, how's the cattle rustling going?" a sweet voice asked.

"Let me tell you, little woman, I wish we were just trying to herd a few hundred head over the border rather than what I'm doing," he told his wife.

"What?" Veronica kidded him. "You mean the Swami hasn't given you the universal truths to solve all our problems yet?"

Carl laughed. "I probably shouldn't have painted Sidney so mystically, but you know I was skeptical that anyone short of a wizard could help. Amazingly, Sidney is helping quite a bit. I feel better about the future of the practice than I have in a long time."

"Well, then the trip's already been worth it. You know I believe in you. You just needed to believe in yourself again. Tell Sidney thanks for me."

Carl realized once again how lucky he was to have Veronica. They talked for a few minutes. Veronica caught him up on the kids, and he gave her a brief run down of what Sidney was having him do with the core values.

"You're right," she said. "That does seem more trouble than rustling livestock. I'll let you get back to it. I just wanted you to remember that we're thinking about you and pulling for you."

Carl smiled to himself. He thought how grateful he was in that moment. *Gratitude.* That would definitely have to be one of his core values. And he instantly knew how to turn that into a specific behavior.

"Veronica, I know I don't say this enough, but I deeply love you. Thank you for being my partner. In good times and bad you make all the difference for me, and for that I am truly, eternally grateful."

There was long pause on the phone. "I love you too," Veronica said softly. "And let me just add that if Sidney taught you to express gratitude that sweetly, then you'll be the top dentist in Madison in no time."

"Thanks again, honey."

"We'll see you tomorrow night, Carl."

"I'll call you when I get to the Albuquerque airport. Talk to you then."

Carl closed his phone slowly and let himself bask in the warmth of Veronica's voice and support. He turned back to his work. Though he'd been stuck on how to recognize and quantify his staff's behaviors so they aligned with the core values, he now knew how to proceed.

On the phone with Veronica, he'd visualized her, and that had made all the difference when he'd expressed his gratitude. He needed to do the same thing with each of his staff members as they performed their duties in the clinic. He started with his lead assistant, formed a picture of her working in the office, and then the professional behaviors he wanted to see started to click.

Carl wrote and wrote, almost forgetting to eat his lunch.

SEVENTEEN

Owning Up to Upsets

A LITTLE AFTER TWO, CARL BOUNDED down the stairs, legal pad in hand, and into the Great Room. Sidney had been reviewing a proof for the new Valuocity Guidebook and stood as Carl approached.

"I'm guessing by the grin on your face that either lunch was exceptionally good, or you made tremendous progress expressing core values as behaviors," Sidney surmised.

"A bit of both and then some. I almost didn't get to Dawn's amazing chicken salad sandwich because I got so wrapped up in my assignment. Also, Veronica called and I used some of your coaching to express my feelings more openly and positively. It really worked!"

"Maybe I should expand my business into marriage counseling," Sidney said with a smile. "Though, I don't think I had much to do with that. Generally, when you feel better about yourself and your situation, things get better around you."

"I'm not sure why I've been down all this time. I didn't realize the kind of prison it put me in," admitted Carl.

"The reason you got so down is you were upset," explained Sidney. "You had an expectation that if you did good work, took great care of your patients, stayed on top of your field and treated your staff right, then you could count on continued growth and success. And for most of your career that was true."

"But then the economy tanked," Carl offered.

"Exactly. Your expectations can no longer be met in the current financial climate. Unfulfilled expectations usually lead to upsets. You were upset, Carl. You thought your success should have gone on forever because you are a good guy and a good dentist. But that's like thinking the bull won't charge you because you're a vegetarian. A lot of business people are going through what you are going through."

"You're right. I see now that I was — still am — upset. And I know when I get upset I become sullen and a little hard to get along with. But honestly, I don't feel as upset anymore, even though my financial situation hasn't changed one whit since we first met."

Sidney held up three fingers. "Carl, an upset has three sources. One is unfulfilled expectations. The second is undelivered communication. And the third is a failed future."

"I understand unfulfilled expectations, but I'm not sure I know what you mean by those last two."

"Well, in San Antonio and again yesterday, you let me know all those things that you were keeping to yourself. Unspoken things, right?"

"Yes," said Carl.

"And after you shared them, those thoughts became less intense and less repetitive?" Sidney prodded.

"Definitely," Carl said, surprised at how right Sidney was.

"Well, what you did was express those undelivered communications and your upset decreased."

Carl nodded slowly in agreement.

"And a failed future," Sidney continued, "that's pretty obvious. You had this clear vision of your future: the money, practice growth, transition, and retirement. You know, the future all dentists dream about. You were well on your way and then you hit a wall. A failed future.

"Carl, you're like most people. When you're upset, you blame others and fault others for your situation. You end up feeling that you're not responsible for your circumstances. And without responsibility, problems never get resolved."

"So, I've spent the last four or five months playing the blame game and letting my practice falter, when I should've been facing my failed future," Carl said, thinking how accurately he'd named himself *Failing Mouse*.

"Pretty much. But your future is far from over, Carl. You're learning how to respond like you should."

"And how should I respond?"

"Like an owner."

EIGHTEEN

Behave Yourself

CARL LOOKED AT SIDNEY QUIZZICALLY. "Okay, I'll bite. How does an owner respond?"

"Like the business is his lifeblood. Or, maybe more fittingly, his bloodline. Carl, you should view your practice as your legacy. What do you want to say through it? What do you want your practice to leave behind? Hopefully, everything that's expressed in your core values."

"Sure," Carl responded. "I want to leave behind a dental practice where I lived my core values: integrity, courage, service, excellence. That would be a great legacy. Those are all characteristics I'd like my practice to represent."

"Good. So how'd you do trying to define your core values so they show up in your staff's behaviors?"

"The first part, describing what my core values mean, that was easy. Defining them as behaviors was a lot trickier."

"How so?" Sidney asked.

"I started out trying to come up with specific behaviors. That was slow going. It occurred to me that I might be doing this backwards, so I visualized specific staff members doing their jobs, and then it really clicked. I thought about integrity and visualized my staff being honest and doing what they say they'd do in the practice. Then I focused on my lead assistant, Karie, and the time clock. It always bothers me when she punches in first thing in the morning and then goes to the bathroom to finish her makeup. She should do that before punching in, but I never call her on it. So, this is what I wrote down."

He picked up his legal pad and read:

> **Integrity:** *Be honest and do what you say you will do.*
>
> **Integrity Behaviors:** *Don't lie about the things you say you will do. If you set a goal or say you will do something, make sure you do it. Don't steal company time. When you punch in to work, don't do personal stuff on my dime.*

Sidney nodded in approval. "Carl, that's exactly what I want. Actually, that's exactly what *you* want. Translating core values into everyday behavior and being able to address them is the key. Keep going."

Carl continued to read from his notes:

> **Courage:** *Do the right thing because it's the right thing to do.*
>
> **Courage Behaviors:** *Don't gossip and don't listen to gossip. If you get upset about something, communicate your upset to the person that can do something about it and don't walk around mad or pouting.*

"Good work," acknowledged Sidney. "Read on!"

Respect: *We treat our patients and each other the way they would like to be treated.*

Respect Behaviors: *Address all patients by their last name unless given permission to do otherwise. Always listen to a patient's communication and paraphrase what they said before responding. Never lecture patients. Always give them the ability to choose whenever possible.*

"A good start on respect for patients," Sidney affirmed and then asked, "Now, what about behaviors of respect among your staff?"

Immediately, Carl visualized some of the office drama. The hygienists were pushy and demanding and often asked for help, but rarely offered any. Carl hated staff meetings when the hygienists complained about the schedule or their instruments. And it really made him crazy with the back and forth bickering that sometimes happened with the other staff.

After a moment or two, Carl wrote down and then read to Sidney:

Respect Behaviors (Staff): *No bickering or complaining to each other about what you are not getting. Be nice to each other. No arguing.*

"Well done, Carl. You are definitely zeroing in on specific behaviors that directly correlate to your core values. That's critical. It will take some time to get them written down for all your core values, but it will be worth it."

Carl was beginning to see the muscle in Sidney's approach. Every issue of discontent in his practice was really based on core values not being present, not being active. When staff did things that didn't embody or express the core values, it caused an upset. Sometimes minor, sometimes major — but it disrupted the mission of his practice. On the flip side, he was getting the picture that when the core values were personified, the practice would perform at a high level and produce results. Excellent results.

"Sidney, I think I finally understand what your slogan about basing your practice on your values is all about. When you don't stay aligned with your core values, things stop working well. What I need in the middle of this economic downturn is everything working at its best."

"That is essential," Sidney emphasized. "You've begun to draft the guidelines that will get your practice realigned and back on track. Now, you need to look a bit more carefully at the behaviors you just wrote to make sure you aren't setting the wrong tone."

"Don't I want to be forceful? I'm the owner. I'm the boss. It's my way or the highway, right?"

Sidney's eyes bored into Carl's. "Let's just remember the question that got you here: Do you want to be right or do you want to be happy?"

NINETEEN

Refine To Define

CARL SHOOK HIS HEAD AS IF TO clear the cobwebs. "Of course I remember what got me here. It's just that you gave me the impression you liked what I'd written for the core behaviors."

"I did, Carl, but it's a starting point. Like a rough draft."

"Well, this is hard work."

"It's hard work because you haven't done this before." Sidney leaned back in his chair. "In our very first conversation you told me about playing basketball. Do you remember when you made the transition from middle school to high school basketball? Was that easy?"

Carl was emphatic. "Hell no! Freshman year was terrible. The coaches were super strict. All we did that first year was run drills and suicides every day. That wasn't fun, and I didn't play that much. I was so frustrated that some days I considered quitting."

"But you didn't, did you? And by the time the coach finally put you in a game, I'll bet you were ready to play. I'll bet you were in great shape and well prepared weren't you?

Preparation and hard work, especially the right kind of hard work, pays off and this will too. So, let's work through refining some of your core behaviors together."

Sidney held out his hand and Carl passed him his notes. "Let's start with what you wrote on Respect Behaviors. You wrote 'no bickering or complaining' and 'no arguing.' First of all you're asking for what you don't want instead of the behaviors you do want to see. Past based, not future based. Second, did you notice anything about the tone of those phrases?"

"The tone is pretty negative. You're right. It feels like I am back to making them wrong again."

"How can you state those behaviors so they are more proactive and positive? How can you state those behaviors so they're future focused? What is it you *do* want?"

Carl thought for a few moments and then said, "We will all respect each other by not complaining to or about one another. We will ask questions to seek solutions to issues that arise."

"Good, Carl. It's future-based and much more positive. You defined what you want to see if respect is present. Now, I want you to remember this question: *How will I measure that behavior?* Don't answer it yet. Just write down the question. You are going to set this up so you can measure whether or not the behaviors you want to see in the practice are actually present. Later, we'll connect this to a process that may put a permanent end to staff complaints."

"I'm all for that!" Carl said.

"Exactly. Now, let's look at Integrity." Sidney read back

over Carl's notes. "I like the phrase 'do what you say you will do.' In my world I call that keeping your word. I want to be surrounded by people that hold this value to be as important as I do. Even though I can't do it 100% of the time, I always try to honor myself as my word. When I give my word, I do everything I can to keep it. I know of no other approach in life that builds and keeps trust like keeping one's word. Again, remember the question: *How will I measure that behavior?*"

Sidney continued. "Listen to what you wrote for Integrity Behaviors. 'Don't steal,' 'don't lie,' and 'don't do personal stuff on my dime.' Again, you are hoping to correct a past behavior, by focusing on the negative — a *don't* behavior instead of the *do* behavior that you really want to see. How would you feel, Carl, if you were an employee and heard all those *don'ts*?"

"Yikes! It sounds awful. I didn't expect it to sound so demeaning." Carl thought for a moment and then suggested, "How about this, Sidney? Keep your time clock records accurately. Complete all personal affairs before clocking in."

"Much better," Sidney said. "You're asking them to support the value of integrity with honest behaviors and you're not assuming that they are trying to cheat you. How about the other part on lying?"

"Yeah, that needs work too. I just want to see my staff being responsible so I don't have to micromanage them all the time. I hate looking over people's shoulders. I want them to follow through with what they say they will do. That's what I meant to say."

"Okay, try again."

Carl closed his eyes and thought for a moment, finally stating, "Follow through and complete the things you say you will do."

"Much more proactive, Carl. You can see how important it is to state exactly the behaviors you want your staff to exhibit — not their misbehaviors. And what's the next thing to consider?"

"How will I measure that behavior!"

Just then Richard came through the kitchen door and waited.

"Excuse me, Carl." Sidney handed back his notes and then walked over to Richard. After a few moments Sidney returned to the fireplace. "Sorry, Carl, ranch business." He looked at his watch. "Why don't you help yourself to a snack in the kitchen and finish your work on core behaviors out on the porch — it's a fine day. We'll meet again for dinner.

"And Carl, when you work on the behaviors, always be thinking about measurement, how to describe behaviors so they can be measured. For example, how can you measure *Being Honest?*

Carl thought about the question. "You can't."

"And why not," asked Sidney. "Why can't you measure honesty?"

Carl considered the question but couldn't come up with an answer. "I'm not sure. It's just something I feel about a person."

"Exactly, it's totally subjective."

"Yeah, that's right," Carl said.

"Try to define your behaviors so they are more objective. You can't measure the subjective but you can measure the objective. Being honest is purely subjective. It's totally an interpretation. But you can define behaviors in a way that is not open to interpretation, where it's not subjective."

"Sidney, I get what you mean but I don't see how to do it."

"Okay, take *Being Honest.* Can you describe a behavior that clearly reflects being honest?"

"How about, not lying?"

"Well, you'd have a tough time trying to measure 'not lying.' How will you know they're not lying? And again, you're focusing on negative behavior. Carl, how else can you measure being honest?"

"I could measure when someone does what they say they will do?" Before he'd finished the thought, a light bulb went off. He was beginning to see how he could define behaviors so they were more objective. Behaviors that could be observed as actual events. Behaviors that reinforced the positive, not prevented the negative. Behaviors that occurred in time and could be measured.

"Wow, Sidney, I think I got it."

"Yes, I can see you do. So go do your homework. And if you finish the assignment or need a break, come down to the bunkhouse. We're having a meeting with a few of the ranch hands to discuss some operational issues. You might find it interesting."

"What will you be discussing?" Carl asked.

"Pulling teeth."

TWENTY

Measure. Measure. Measure.

SIDNEY LEFT WITH RICHARD. Carl went into the kitchen and found a pitcher of iced tea and corn muffins sitting on the counter. He filled a tall glass with tea, put three muffins on a plate and stuffed a napkin in his shirt pocket.

He made his way to the porch and dropped into a handmade rocking chair. He sat still for several moments, enjoying the stillness of the mountains and the warmth of the sun. He took a deep breath, exhaled, and sipped the minty tea. For the first time in months, he felt less anxious. He was actually feeling hopeful about the future. He did not know exactly where values based behaviors would lead, but he sensed he was on the right path.

Picking up his pencil, he started thinking about his core value of excellence. Carl still struggled with this one. He thought he always strived for excellence in everything he did clinically, but what behaviors would he look for if the staff displayed the same commitment to excellence?

He didn't have a ready answer. He gazed up at the blue sky interrupted with scattered clouds. He stared at the various billowy white shapes and let his mind wander. One reminded him of a kangaroo, another of a maxillary first molar. One cloud in the distance looked like his Porsche. He stared at it drifting along the horizon. The thought of having to sell this prized car if he couldn't rescue his practice brought back a spasm of anxiety.

He refocused on his work. *What behaviors would reveal excellence in the practice and how would I measure them?*

The more he pondered, the more he realized he had no operational definition of excellence. How in the world would he be able to measure excellent behaviors? What behaviors or actions would indicate that both he and the staff were excellent and how would he measure that?

He leaned back in the rocking chair and considered those questions. *I know*, he thought, *it would be really excellent if all of us would set goals for ourselves and achieve the goals we set. That would be excellent, and that would be a measurable behavior.* He quickly copied these ideas down on his legal pad.

Following this train of thought he asked himself aloud, "What is not excellent that I wish were excellent?"

He stared back up at the clouds, as though looking for an answer. As Sidney pointed out yesterday, there were few things that were truly excellent in his practice. One thing he knew for sure, he did not like the absence of communication in the office. That was a problem that needed to be remedied.

What would excellent communication behaviors look like and how could they be measured? What would I really like to see? Carl reflected on his upsets and complaints about communication. He wondered what wasn't happening in communication that got him so upset, that had the whole staff in an uproar.

Then it hit him.

What he really wanted was his staff to deliver communications to the appropriate individuals. He hated hearing about problems third hand or having to deal with gossip. In his notes, he wrote the following:

> ***EXCELLENCE***
> *Communications: Staff members deliver communications to the appropriate person or persons that need to hear them. No triangulating and no gossip. Communications are delivered responsibly and without blame.*

This identified excellent communication that was observable. And it was clearly measurable. *You either gossip or you don't. You either take your issue to the person the issue is with or you don't. You're either responsible in your communication or you're not.* He was getting a better grasp on defining behaviors that could be observed and measured, and not open to interpretation.

He considered his core value of Integrity. He wrote down, *Keep your word.* He figured he could keep track of this behavior although he wasn't sure exactly how to measure it yet.

He wrote:

> *Keep your time clock records accurate; perform personal affairs before clocking in for the day.*
>
> *Ask permission to use company resources for personal use such as toothbrushes, stamps, the Internet and any other resource the practice pays for.*

Those things were measurable. Carl was on a roll. He had an easier time coming up with behaviors for the next few values.

After an hour of good progress, he looked down at his watch, realizing he would have time to catch the bunkhouse meeting. Leaving his pad and pen on the small table next to the rocking chair, he ambled in the direction of the bunk house, wondering if ranch business was anything like the dental business.

Sidney had said they'd be discussing 'pulling teeth.' He'd understood that as dental humor. Any hard job could be described as pulling teeth. Then, again, maybe Sidney had to do extractions on some of his horses. Now, that sounded tricky. Not something that came up in Madison. He conjured up an image of a horse in one of his dental chairs.

The thought made him smile.

TWENTY-ONE

Request for the Best

THE PATH TO THE BUNK HOUSE consisted of crushed red gravel and Carl's shoes crunched noisily as he walked. Tall pines surrounded the two-story building and the rich scent coaxed Carl to inhale deeply. As he approached the entrance, he looked through the window and saw Richard and several other ranch hands seated around a long table.

Before Carl could knock on the weather-beaten screen door he heard Sidney call out, "Come on in." The men were sitting in ladder-back chairs around the darkly stained, heavily used rectangular table. On the wall at the head of the table was a large white board where Sidney was standing.

"Welcome, Carl. Let me introduce you to my top hands," he said, motioning to each of the men around the table. "Rick here is point man for our horses. Juan is in charge of building and maintenance and Daniel is accountable for livestock. And, you know Richard."

Carl nodded to each. All the men showed clear signs of having worked outdoors for most of their lives. Rugged skin, dark tans, quite a few more wrinkles than most folks their age. Each smiled to Carl as they were introduced, and, as only a dentist might notice, he saw that they all had pretty good teeth.

"Take a seat, anywhere, Carl."

He took a seat at the far end of the table. On the walls around the room, notices were tacked up about calf branding, training of the new horses and the maintenance schedules for the stable, the bunk house and the ranch vehicles. Near the doorway a large poster read:

VALUES RANCH
HARD WORK
COMMUNICATION
TEAMWORK
COURAGE
PROFITABILITY
WE LIVE OUR VALUES

Carl immediately recognized the list as core values. It was heartening to see that Sidney practiced his own preaching. He looked closely at the list. He hadn't really considered the ranch as a real business; he thought it was more a hobby for Sidney. It secretly pleased Carl to see that some of the core values were the same ones he'd come up with.

After the introductions, Sidney turned back to the white board and completed the list he'd started before Carl's arrival.

Current Issues to Solve

1. Extra hands for cattle drive
2. Summer vacation schedules
3. New feed supplier
4. Equipment breakdowns

At the top of the white board in stick-on letters read the following:

Requests / Promises / Who / By When

"If you guys don't mind I'm going to bring Carl up to speed. He's visiting the ranch to work on some issues in his dental practice and I want him to see how we operate within our core values.

"Carl, what do you see up here?"

"Well," Carl paused, a bit surprised to be put on the spot. "It looks like you've got a list of problems to solve, and you're looking to figure out who's going to do what and by when."

"Good. And what else do you notice?"

"Um, that's all I see."

"Do you see any similarities between the ranching business and the dental business? We both have issues and conflicts that center around people and equipment. We both have procedures that need to be carried out, issues with vendors. For you it's dental supplies, dental equipment and patients. With us it's horse and cattle supplies, ranch equipment and customers. We both need to manage people, supplies and profitability. Almost all businesses have similar issues to handle. It doesn't matter whether it's ranching or dentistry; you either manage your business or you go out of business."

Carl nodded.

"Carl, you've made it clear to me you dislike having to micromanage your staff."

"Sure do. If someone says they will do something I hate to nag them to get it done."

"Well, we all do. In fact, that's the beauty of values-based behaviors. Since one of your core values is integrity, a behavior you expect is that people will do what they say they will do. So, a system of requests and promises is a good measure of integrity."

Sidney wrote the word *results* on the white board. "Carl, consider this. There are lots of results you would like to produce in your practice, right? So, how do you produce results?"

"I am not sure I follow you, Sydney. When I need to do something I just do it."

"Okay, that's one way. But there are results that you want your staff to produce and behaviors you want your staff to display. So, how do you get them to produce results?"

"Well, I tell them what I want done," Carl said.

"And then what?"

"Then I wait, and hope they do it."

"Yes, and having hope as your business plan, how's that working? It's stressful and unfulfilling, I'm guessing. Living in hope won't produce consistent results. The one thing

I've learned is that to be successful you don't rely on hope — you rely on commitment."

Sidney looked to all his ranch hands. "On the ranch we rely on commitment." Rick, Juan, Daniel and Richard all nodded. "Commitment means giving your word and keeping it. It's a promise. Around here, when we use the word *request*, it means I am asking you for a promise."

Sidney pointed to the stick-on letters. "We use a system of requests and promises to produce results. The way it works is anyone around the ranch can identify some action that needs to happen and can make a request of anyone else. A request is not a demand, and the person to whom the request is directed can do one of three things. They can accept the request, decline the request, or they can make a counter to the request."

Carl was wishing he'd brought his legal pad and pen to write some of this down, but he stayed focused as Sidney continued.

"When someone accepts a request, that is an actual promise for action and all promises for action have due dates. One of your jobs as the owner and manager of your practice is to always move the action forward. Specific due dates help make that happen. Any questions, Carl?"

"Yes," said Carl. "What happens if people don't deliver on their promises when they say they will?"

"That's the beauty of a values-based business. When someone is truly responsible for their promise, and if something interferes with them fulfilling their promise, they need to communicate that to you and ask for support. That is integrity in action."

"Well, what if it happens all the time?" Carl asked. "I have a receptionist that always promises stuff and never gets it done, but she always has great reasons why."

Sidney didn't answer for a few moments. "There are several things to consider. Is she saying 'Yes' when she should be saying 'No' in order to tell you what you want to hear? Is she saying 'Yes' to a request she does not have the resources or capacity to fulfill? Can she honestly say 'No' without fear that you will be angry with her?"

"I think so," Carl said.

"I hope so," Sidney said emphatically, "Remember, an employee cannot honestly say 'Yes' if they cannot say 'No.' If you have a dedicated employee that produces results, then this system will work. If you have an employee who is not in alignment with your values and who does not produce the results they promise, then your performance reviews will reveal the weakness and you have a choice to make."

"You mean I have to fire that person?"

"Not necessarily. We'll talk about being at choice and performance reviews later. But for now the important thing to grasp is the basic elements of this system."

"I'd love to see the system in action," Carl said in earnest.

"That sounds like a reasonable request. Gentlemen, let's show our guest from Madison how Taos gets the job done."

TWENTY-TWO

Ranch Style

SIDNEY POINTED TO THE FIRST ITEM on the list written on the white board.

Extra hands for cattle drive

"We've already discussed the need for extra hands on the cattle drive. Rick you said you need five more hands to safely handle the round-up, correct?"

"Yes, sir," replied Rick.

Rick sat directly to Carl's left. He was the prototypical cowboy wearing a plaid work-shirt, jeans and a red kerchief around his neck. He had straight black hair combed back and a bushy black mustache that buried his upper lip and trailed down to his jawbone.

"So Rick, what needs to happen next?" Sidney asked.

"I can call the association and see who is available for temporary work."

"Alright, can you make the call, find out who is

available and what the total costs will be including temporary liability insurance? And can you make sure the extra costs will stay within our quarterly budget?"

"Yes, sir, I can."

"If it pencils out, hire the men and send out the confirmations that they will be here when we need them and get the forms filled out and signed. Can you do this by next Wednesday at noon?"

"Sure boss. Consider it done. What if it takes us over budget?"

"Then we may need to make adjustments. If that's the case, bring the figures to me by noon on Wednesday. We can decide then. Do you need any support to get this done?"

"Well, I could use some help from Juan to cover my duties at the coral for about two to three hours on Tuesday while I get this done. Juan, can you cover for me?"

"Sure," Juan said, "but I'll need to adjust my hours so I won't have to put in for overtime like you asked. Is that okay, Rick?"

"Yup. Thanks, Juan. Boss, we'll get it done."

Sidney went up to the board and wrote under the line Requests/Promises/Who/By When:

> **Request:** Hire five hands for round-up (Sidney)
> **Promise:** Hire five hands for drive (Rick, Wednesday Noon)

"Okay," Sidney continued down the list. "Vacation schedules are next. What's the issue?"

Juan spoke up. "Boss," he said, "I made a request for my vacation schedule that was declined. I'm not happy about that. I really need that week off to attend a family gathering."

Richard responded to him. "Juan, you know the policy. No two ranch hands can be off the same week. That week we're busy and we can't afford to be short two hands."

"I know things come up sometimes that require extra effort to figure out, Richard," Sidney interjected. "If Juan can come up with a plan to get his duties covered for the week with the other hands and not cost us overtime would you be willing to approve the time off?"

"Sure, boss, but we don't have a lot of time to get this done."

"Okay, Richard, can you make a request?" Sidney prompted.

"Juan," said Richard, "if you come up with a plan that is workable and doesn't cost us overtime or put us over budget, then I'd be willing to approve the time off. But, I need to see your plan on paper, and pretty soon. When can you get that to me?"

"I need to figure out what needs to be done and talk around to see who can cover for me." Juan paused to consider the time this would take. "I guess I'll need a few days. Can I get it to you by the end of the day on Wednesday?"

Richard was quick with his reply. "No good, Juan, I really need it sooner. Can I see it 6:30 AM Tuesday over coffee? Shouldn't take long if you cover all the bases."

"Agreed." Juan nodded. "Thanks for letting me try to work this out."

Sidney went to the board and wrote:

Request: Reschedule vacation time (Juan)
Promise: Vacation solution for Richard to approve (Juan, Tuesday 6:30 AM)

Carl marveled at how the issues were addressed and being handled so efficiently. The potentially upsetting issue with Juan was handled maturely and effectively with requests and promises. Carl also appreciated how skillful Sidney was at helping Richard work out the request he needed to make of Juan to help him resolve his problem with the schedule. It was Juan's problem and he needed to take responsibility to solve it.

Carl immediately saw the value in tracking requests, promises and by whens. He realized he could make a form to use for this. He would have the office manager write down all the requests, promises and by whens and post them in the staff lounge. Then they could review them each day at the morning meeting. He loved the idea that everyone would be aware of each other's promises. And by making them public, it would essentially raise the bar for everyone's performance.

The meeting continued with Sidney going through the remaining items on the agenda. Each issue was handled smoothly and without conflict. Carl saw how this would raise efficiencies and take the pressure off him for nagging staff. Carl looked back up at the Core Values sign again.

He thought to himself, *I need to make one of those signs for the office and include Communication as one of my core values.* He realized that he valued open and honest communication, and this value was not being honored in the office. Now he had a tool to use to make more effective communication possible.

He was so deep in thought he didn't notice the meeting had ended. The jostling of chairs against the wooden floor got his attention.

"Come on, Carl," Sidney said, motioning him to the door. "Let's get some ice tea. Making requests and promises is thirsty business."

As they walked back along the path, Sidney asked, "Did you find that valuable?"

"Where do I begin? It was incredibly eye-opening. First, I saw that responsible people can communicate without constant bickering, even with difficult situations. When Juan had a complaint about his vacation request, the complaint was turned into a request for action instead of bickering. I like the way you urged Richard to make his request for Juan rather than you having to step in to make it. The process was very effective. I can certainly use that in the office when people complain. I can ask them to make a request. That will be a great help."

"Glad you saw it as worthwhile. Richard is an excellent foreman, but, like all of us, he gets overwhelmed when he has too much to do. He takes on a lot of responsibility around here. I see my role as a leader to help him grow in his ability to make requests. One of the things you need to consider is what requests you need to make to whom when you get back to the office. And, Carl, when you can make big requests of the staff, you'll notice that your confidence will grow. When you can make it safe for your staff to make requests, their confidence will grow too. That will be a win-win for everybody."

"I can see how this process allows trust within the office to develop as well."

"Exactly." Sidney checked his watch. "We've still got a couple hours before dinner. How's your homework coming?"

"I'm getting there. I think I've got some more ideas after watching your meeting."

"Good. You know, I'd like you to take some time to write down a few requests you'll make when you get back to your office. Can you do that too?"

"Sidney, that sounds like a *request*." Carl chuckled.

"You're catching on to how we do business on the Values Ranch. Hopefully, it'll follow you all the way back to Madison."

"It will," said Carl. "And that's a *promise!*"

CHAPTER 23

You Can't Go Back

CARL WAS FAMISHED WHEN HE ENTERED the kitchen on the dot at seven. Dawn was behind the stove stirring a large pot with steam spilling out. She waved 'Hello,' smiled and then turned to check the oven. Sidney wasn't there yet, so Carl walked up to the island in the middle of the kitchen.

"Smells good, Dawn. What's for dinner?"

"Last night you had elk stew. Tonight, you're having another house specialty, elk ribs. And they are looking ready."

Just then Sidney walked into the kitchen. He inhaled deeply. "Aaaaaah, after a busy day, that's just what the doctor ordered. Elk ribs! Wait till you taste them, Carl. They're fabulous."

They sat down at the table. Only two places were set with large cloth napkins. Sidney picked up his napkin. "Gets to be a little messy," he said smiling.

"Aren't Dawn and Richard going to join us?" Carl asked.

"No, Saturday nights they like to go into Taos to dance."

Carl tried to picture Richard dancing. It was a bit of a stretch, but he thought he might be able to pull off some Fierce Eagle moves.

Carl and Sidney dug into the ribs. After their initial hunger was appeased, they started to talk. They didn't discuss dentistry or Carl's practice; they talked about the greater economic climate. Sidney kept using the term the 'New Economy' until Carl pinned him down on what that meant.

Sidney explained, "In most of our past recessions, the U.S. could export its way out of the problem. But with this particular recession being global, with most countries lacking hard currency or credit, it's very different. Easy cash. Easy credit. Those things are not going to come back. And, honestly, they shouldn't. We shouldn't build our economy around bubbles. The new economy has to be built on value.

"That's why it's so important to build your practice on your core values. They're immune to external conditions. They're unchangeable. They're consistent. They're constant. No matter what changes happen in the economy, your values will keep you stable and on purpose."

Carl nodded his approval. He was beginning to see what Sidney was really about. It was kind of like the movie *Field of Dreams*: if you build it, they will come. If you built something people value, the word will get out, and they'll show up. But, it had to be something they trusted, something core to their lives. It was an important insight for Carl.

Soon the ribs were gone and the two were draining their ice teas.

"Well," Carl said, "I've still got lots of questions about your meeting with the ranch hands today. I'd like to understand better how you accomplished so much in a meeting using requests and promises."

"Good. Let's meet by the fireplace in twenty minutes. Bring your work, and I'll bring us a couple beers."

"Wow." Carl smiled. "I didn't even have to make a request for a beer."

"Good service often times means anticipating a request." Sidney rose from the table. "And good service is something I value."

"I'll drink to that," Carl said as he left to get his notes.

TWENTY-FOUR

Afraid of Commitment

SIDNEY WAS POURING TWO TALL GLASSES with Sahalie IPA, a Washington State microbrew, when Carl came down the stairs. He handed one to Carl. "Here's a request I'm happy to fulfill. Cheers."

Carl took a long drink. "That's good. Thanks. I'll mark it off your promise list."

Both took seats on the sofa, Carl flipping a page on his legal pad and clicking his pen, ready to take notes.

"Sidney, tell me more about this request-promise system. It was amazing how efficiently your meeting with the ranch hands went."

"Carl, most meetings are meaningless. They generally consist of people exchanging information, and information has no power."

"Pardon? Isn't that what meetings are for? Don't you need to exchange information?"

"Yes and no. Most meetings push information back and forth. But the information usually comes as opinions, complaints, judgments, assessments, stories or reasons. There are a thousand and one ways to communicate information. The problem is that information doesn't produce results."

"How can you say information doesn't produce results?" Carl asked with a frown.

"Simple," said Sidney, "information doesn't produce results."

"Then, how could you ever make an informed decision?" asked Carl. "Information is valuable."

"I'm not denying that information has value. I'm just saying that information alone doesn't necessarily change behaviors, or produce results. Look, everybody has information about the importance of exercise and diet, but how many people do it? Everybody knows not to spend more money than they make, but how many folks in our country do that? Everyone knows telling the truth is always the best thing, but how many people follow that axiom? Everyone has the information to make good decisions, to take action, but how many really do?"

"Okay," Carl conceded. "I see your point, but what about dental school and all the information we learned?"

"How much of the information you learned in dental school do you use today? Information generally has a pretty short shelf life. Information has no real power. Sure, it will make you smarter. Sure, you will understand something better. But in terms of producing results, it has little impact."

Sidney paused and took another swig of his beer. Carl

was poised to write something, but he couldn't quite figure out what. He was confused by Sidney's assertion that information had no impact. "Sidney, how can you run a business — or your life — without information?"

"Like I said before, information is important, but just supplying heaps of information to people isn't enough." Sidney leaned forward in his seat. "Tell me, Carl, how do you lead your staff meetings? Do you try to convince, explain, give reasons, threaten, cajole, or plead with your staff? Do you give them the numbers about production, collection, new patients?

"If you're like most dentists, you expect information to stimulate actions that produce results — which it rarely does. You expect job descriptions will motivate staff to perform. You expect their paychecks will make them work hard. You expect numbers and statistics to solve problems. But information in any form does little to generate effective action."

Carl considered himself an information junkie, so what he said next was more a challenge than a question. "So, what does deliver the action that produces results then?"

"Commitment!" Sidney exclaimed.

"But you still need information to make a decision, don't you?" asked Carl.

"Of course you need information to make decisions. I didn't say information wasn't important. I just said that information alone doesn't produce action, and you need action to produce results. Results don't happen spontaneously, they require action to happen."

Carl rubbed his temples. "Let's see if I've got this right. Information by itself doesn't generate results. You need action to produce results. And, commitment is what generates action? Is that right?"

"Yes, commitment is the catalyst that generally ignites effective action." Sidney paused and then continued, "Carl, if you listen closely to those forms of communication that deliver information — reasons, explanations, judgments, complaints, and so on — the verbs used are past tense. They're *descriptive* in nature. As a manager, you want to generate action that produces a specific result. When you start out to generate a result, that result lives in the future. The way I see it, you need to use language that is future based, not past based. You need to speak in a way that makes that future happen. Information doesn't get us to the future, it only gets us to the past."

Sidney continued slowly now, wanting to make certain Carl was understanding. "A promise is a commitment spoken. A request is asking another for a promise. The more specific the request or the promise, the more powerful. The more time anchored the request or the promise, the more powerful. A request and a promise are the language of commitment. And what's more, Carl, if you listen closely, a promise uses future tense verbs. A promise says, 'I give my word to a future and I will honor myself as my word.' What could be more powerful than that?"

Carl was taking notes furiously. Sidney waited for him to catch up. "Did you get all that?"

Reading partly from his notes, Carl replied, "A promise

initiates action. A promise focuses action on a particular future. A promise is honoring yourself as your word. Given that one of my core values is integrity, this all fits together. I think I'm beginning to get it, but can you give me an example?"

"Sure. Let's use exercise as an example. You and I could talk for hours about the importance of exercise. We could exchange information: cardiovascular benefits, increased metabolism, prevention of chronic diseases, better self-image, more stamina, and even better sex."

Carl couldn't help but smile.

"None of this information will get you to exercise. It will make you smarter about exercise. You will have a better understanding, more reasons, more information about why you should exercise, but it won't produce the result of you exercising. It won't get you to the gym."

"I understand that, but I'm unclear why information doesn't prompt action. It would for me."

"Information is talking about something. It doesn't have you be responsible. It doesn't promote commitment. Information illuminates, but it doesn't motivate."

It would motivate me, thought Carl. *Why not everyone?*

"Carl, let's say I ask you to make a promise about exercising for the next six months. Then you let me hold you accountable for keeping your word. Now, you are responsible to me. You've made a commitment and that will provoke action."

"Okay, keep going."

"A promise made to yourself has no power. That's

called a New Year's resolution. Lots of promises are made on December 31st at midnight, but few are kept. Why?"

"I'm not sure." Carl reflected back to his New Year's resolution about diet which didn't last through the next day when the bowl games started and the clam dip came out.

"It's actually pretty straightforward," Sidney explained. "For a promise to have power it needs to be made to someone that you give permission to hold you to your promise. I call this other person a 'committed listener.'"

Carl nodded, affirming he understood.

"Now, a good committed listener makes sure that what you promise can and will be fulfilled. That's what I do as a coach for my clients. I listen and interact with them around their promises. I hold them to account to deliver on their word. I look from the point of view of 'Can I promise their promise to someone else?'

"If we look back on the exercise example, I would listen to your promise so that I believe you really mean what you say. That you are truly committed to what you promise. If I think your promise is half-hearted, as a committed listener, I need to challenge your resolve."

"Sidney, how do you know the promise is really a legitimate promise?"

"A powerful promise is pretty specific. 'I promise to get in shape this year' is a pretty weak promise. But 'I promise to go to the gym four times a week, exercise aerobically for 30 minutes each session, do 100 crunches, and begin weight training with a trainer three times a week' is a much more powerful promise."

Carl wrote a few more notes. "Tell me if I got it right. Information has little power to inspire action."

"Right."

"And you need someone who is responsible for their word and committed to doing what he or she says. Someone you trust will honor themselves as their word."

"Very good, Carl."

"You need someone who will hold the person making the promise accountable to give and keep their word."

"Yes, that's right."

"The more specific and more time-anchored the promise, the more powerful the promise."

"Carl, you've got it. Can you see how this would work in your practice? Remember, a request is asking another for a promise."

"Absolutely, I can stop trying to convince my staff of what to do and simply make requests," Carl said.

"That's the idea." Sidney said. "Now, can you apply those concepts to a situation in your office?"

"Give me a second." Carl tapped his pen on his notepad as he thought. "Instead of badgering my front desk to call patients 48 hours in advance in order to decrease no shows, and having to make her feel guilty for not doing it, I simply could make a standing request."

"What would that request be?" Sidney asked.

"That all patients are always called 48 hours in advance to confirm their appointment."

"And if your front desk can't follow through on that request, what do you do?"

Carl looked around uncomfortably. "I was hoping your system of requests and promises would clear up these problems."

"It certainly can," Sidney said, "but, what if it doesn't work with an employee. Then what will you do?"

"Yell at them. Fire them. Or just roll my eyes and hope tomorrow will be a better day."

"None of those are very good options, Carl." Sidney looked at his watch. "It's getting late, so, I'll give you an idea to mull over tonight."

"What is it?"

"If an employee is not responding to requests, not performing up to par, don't dump them — develop them."

"Develop them?"

"Yup. See you at seven for breakfast."

TWENTY-FIVE

Take Off the Training Wheels

CARL AWOKE AT 6:15 FEELING REFRESHED. He'd left the window open about an inch and the crisp mountain air had invigorated him. Thinking about everything he'd learned on the ranch, he took his time getting ready for the day. He felt upbeat. Something about reconnecting with his core values pushed aside much of the self doubt he'd been experiencing. Yesterday's work on behavior and core values was the key. He could feel that his practice, firmly grounded in core values, would be much more effective — and successful. Carl was eager to get going.

When he entered the kitchen, Sidney was on his cell phone looking out the window, talking softly. Dawn called from the gas range, "Good morning, Carl. What would you like for breakfast? Eggs? French toast? Bacon? Ham? Wheat toast or a plain bagel?"

Dawn's openness and friendliness, the extent of her

hospitality, impressed Carl. He felt appreciated and really welcome. He wondered if he could get his front office staff to make their clients feel this welcome. He realized it was one thing to offer someone French toast and another having a tooth drilled, but he knew that patients (or customers) knew when there was genuine care being provided. That kind of care was at the heart of good service.

He answered Dawn heartily, "I'd love to have scrambled eggs and ham and a toasted bagel, please."

"Coming right up," Dawn said with a smile.

Sidney ended his call. "Good morning, Carl. Sleep well?"

"Very well. Thanks. I didn't even let your cliff-hanger comment about not dropping staff, but developing them, keep me awake."

"I'm pleased to know that you're able to compartmentalize. We'll get to developing staff in a bit. Right now I want to hear about the technical aspects of your practice."

While Dawn prepared breakfast, they talked shop. Carl expounded on veneers, CEREC, digital imaging and the new composite materials he was using. He discussed his last three years taking all nine courses with Kois, his initial work with Frank Spears eight years ago, and his participation with Pankey after purchasing his practice. Carl went into recent implant programs and training up in Canada, as well as the Seattle Study Club he'd been part of for seven years.

When they'd finished eating, Sidney changed the tenor of the conversation. "It's obvious that you enjoy the clinical side of your practice. You've been involved with some great programs. Now, how do you like running your practice? How do you like the management side of the business?"

The enthusiasm that had brightened Carl's features when he spoke of his clinical expertise vanished. He frowned. "Honestly, I don't think I'm very good at it. I'd rather deal with porcelain than people."

"You're not alone," Sidney remarked. "You and most dentists don't know how to manage. You were never taught how to run a business in dental school, and the hardest thing about running a business is managing people. Most dentists think management is about control and telling the staff what and how to do their jobs. And that's not even close to what it takes."

"Well, what is management then?" asked Carl.

"Management has two sides. One certainly is producing results through others. The other, which is often missed, is developing people through work."

"Is that what you were talking about last night — about developing them rather than firing them?"

"Yes. Ideally, management's job is to help people grow as human beings. To become more able, more confident, and more successful in their own right." Sidney stopped for a moment and looked Carl in the eyes. "Do you think you are developing your staff as employees or do you look at them as objects to help you do your dentistry and make you money?"

"I don't think I use them that way," Carl said, defensively.

"No?" Sidney challenged. "Do you know where your staff need education or training beyond just getting the immediate job done? Do you know the personal goals or aspirations of each of your staff? Do you know what their dreams are? Do you know what you need to do for each one of them to have their lives be more fulfilling?"

Carl couldn't look at Sidney when he answered. "No, not really. I know my front desk really well because she's been with me for 12 years. My hygienist has been with me almost that long. As for the other staff, we're friendly, but I really don't know much about them."

"What if part of your job as manager was to improve their lives through work? Can you see how much different you'd be with them at work?"

Sidney didn't wait for an answer and continued. "Why do you think staff members leave or under-perform in most dental practices? If you think it's about the money, you'd be wrong. Sometimes they have to leave for family reasons, like their husband gets a job in another location. But most of the time they leave because the dentist just doesn't care about them as people. They feel undervalued, unfulfilled."

Carl began to think of the parade of assistants that had come and gone in his office. He couldn't even remember some of their names. And his second hygiene position, he couldn't recall if it was three or four hygienists that had come and gone in the last five years.

Sidney continued. "All I'm really saying is the reason there's such a high turnover rate in dental practices is dentists aren't committed to the growth and development of their staff. They care about results, which is fine, but they don't see the value of developing people and how that would impact their practice."

"How do you develop people?"

"How do you develop your own children, Carl?"

Carl thought for a few moments. "Veronica and I try to teach them solid values and give them opportunities to grow."

"Exactly. You have a commitment to your kids that they develop as human beings, become better people, stay out of trouble, get a good education, become productive, be happy and fulfilled. What if you were to apply the same commitment and intention to your staff?"

"I'm not raising a staff. I'm training one."

"That's what you do to circus animals, Carl. Do you want a staff that just jumps through the hoops when you're around because they'll get some reward for looking good? Or would you rather have a staff as fully invested in the welfare of the practice as you are? That means they have to grow along with the practice. You have to provide them opportunities. You have to establish the core values they'll agree to support. When you commit to your staff's development, it generates relationships of trust, kinship and affinity. With this kind of relationship in place, you can develop a management system where you have partners, not payroll players. Then you get buy-in and results."

Carl held up his hand as if to stop the avalanche of ideas coming from Sidney. "Hold on. There's only so much my brain can hold this early on a Sunday morning. I see what you're saying, but I need some time to digest it. Some of it is fuzzy, while other aspects are starting to crystallize."

"That's what you call an insight," Sidney explained. "An insight is much more than information. Actually it is a phenomenon. All of a sudden that which has always been there, somehow becomes clear, distinguished, and fully comprehensible. An insight changes everything all at once."

"Well, this feels like a storm, and it's raining insights so hard that I'm not able to see the horizon."

Sidney laughed. "I understand. I have been accused of infecting a client or two with *insight-itis*."

Carl smiled weakly. "Yeah, I think that's what I've got."

"Don't worry," Sidney said. "A cup of really strong coffee and a short break usually relieves the symptoms. Let's meet in the Great Room in half an hour."

TWENTY-SIX

Hope, Prayer and Job Descriptions

A HALF HOUR LATER WHEN THEY reconvened by the fireplace, Sidney continued their discussion on management.

"Most dentists set up management by job description. Many have purchased thick manuals with hundreds of pages defining each job and describing in great detail the actions each staff should individually take to get his or her job done."

Carl nodded and said proudly, "Yup. Got one from a former consultant. I've been using it for the last eight years, and I have the staff update their duties each year."

"How has it worked?" asked Sidney.

"Well, it seemed to work fine until last year when the practice started to slip. Then, because we don't have as many patients coming through the door, there just isn't as much work to do."

"You see, Carl, job descriptions are only good for a practice that isn't in the middle of a recession. Their job descriptions don't help now do they?"

"No, not so much."

"If I remember correctly, your core values are *integrity, courage, respect, excellence, improvement, service* and *profit*. Is that right Carl?"

"Yes, though, I think I'd like to add *communication* as well."

"Okay, that's good. Now, is there any direct connection between your job descriptions and your core values?"

Carl closed his eyes and ran through some of the job descriptions he used. After a few moments he opened his eyes and shook his head. "No, I don't see a strong correlation."

"Well, that's pretty typical. Now, work with me on this one. We're going to switch gears for a moment. Carl, you have two teenage children."

"Jonathon and Amy," Carl offered proudly.

Sidney smiled. "Do you consider yourself a good Dad?"

"I like to think so. My kids mean the world to me."

"I believe you. Now, do you have a manual that has a job description for you as a Dad?" Sidney asked.

Carl laughed. "Of course not."

"Has your job changed every year as a Dad?"

"Pretty much."

"So, even if you had a Dad job description, it would be obsolete quickly. It would be outdated every year. Right?"

Carl nodded.

"So how do you know what to do as a Dad even though you don't have a job description? How do you know what actions to take even though it isn't written down somewhere?"

Carl quietly considered what he did as a parent before he answered. "I don't know, Sidney. I just do what I think is right and what feels right and that's how I make my choices. And, if I'm not sure, I ask Veronica. I don't think I need a job description to be a good parent."

"Then why does your staff need job descriptions to be good performers?"

Carl was stuck for an answer. "I'm not sure. I never thought about it. I've just done what the consultants told me to do, and what everyone else around me is doing."

"Then, how do you know what to do as a parent if you don't have a job description? What guides you in your decision making? What enables you to go above and beyond to make sure your kids are safe and make sound decisions?" Sidney pressed.

"Well, it's just how I am as a parent," responded Carl. "I feel I'm responsible. I provide for my kids. I'm the one responsible that they grow up healthy, stay out of trouble, do their best, get educated, and contribute something positive to the world."

"So *you* are responsible, and from owning that responsibility you understand what your job is. Do I have that right, Carl?"

"I never thought about it quite that way, but yeah, that's right."

"Now, think about having a staff that is as responsible for their jobs as you are for being a parent. What would your practice look like if that were the case?"

As Carl answered, he sensed something wonderful happening. "What would it look like? It would be unbelievable if staff were that responsible. I wouldn't have to manage them. They would manage themselves."

"So, Carl, if staff were responsible for their jobs in the same way you are responsible for parenting, would that be an expression of your core values?"

"Absolutely! It all connects to integrity, respect, improvement, service and communication," Carl responded with genuine enthusiasm. "I can see how responsibility enables people to do the right thing, make the right decisions and take appropriate actions as a parent would. My big question is how do I get my staff to be responsible?"

Sidney's response stopped Carl cold. "*You* can't!"

TWENTY-SEVEN

Choosing and Losing (or Winning)

CARL'S JAW FROZE OPEN.

"Look," Sidney explained, hoping to ease Carl's distress, "*you* can't get another person to be responsible. They have to do it themselves. There's no secret formula, no simple elixir, no magic wand. People have to choose to be responsible or not. In fact, responsibility begins with choice."

"How so?"

"Carl, what do you always have control over? What are you in command of?"

"I'm not sure what you're getting at."

"Let me give you an example. Did you ever think about cheating when you were in school?" Sidney asked.

"Sure, yeah, why?"

"Give me a specific incident."

One time stood out in Carl's mind. "I was in pharmacology my second year of dental school. My roommate really knew his stuff, and I didn't. We sat next to each other in class. On our first exam, I knew I was in trouble by the third question. I remember having this conversation in my head about whether to look at my roommate's answers."

"So, what did you do?"

"It makes me sad to say, but I copied two of his answers. Then, I started having second thoughts. I stopped looking at his paper and did the best I could on my own."

"What made you choose not to cheat anymore?"

"It wasn't right. It was dishonest."

"But," Sidney prodded, "wasn't there a payoff to cheating? You'd get a better grade."

"Maybe," Carl admitted," though it would cost me sleep. My conscience would make me pay. And if I got caught, I could've been tossed from dental school. The costs were too high."

"So, in essence, you made a choice based on costs and payoffs," Sidney said. "What was different before and after you made that choice not to continue cheating?"

"Well, before I made the choice, I was uncertain. I wasn't sure what I should do or should not do. I wasn't thinking clearly. I felt torn between getting a decent grade and dealing with the consequences of failing. I was more worried about my position in class standing than honoring my values. The uncertainty made me feel anxious and indecisive."

"What about after you made your choice?"

"I didn't have to worry. I no longer had mixed feelings. I felt a whole lot better about myself. More at peace."

"So once you made a choice, once you chose to take the test without cheating, once you considered the cost and payoff of cheating, you felt better, more confident?"

"Well, I was more relaxed. I didn't feel like a thief."

"Okay, Carl, in thinking about this example, wouldn't you want your staff to come from 'choice' rather than being told what to do?"

"Sure. I'd love for them to always do the right thing."

"Wouldn't we all," Sidney remarked with a smile. "That's the key to building a sense of responsibility in your staff. Choice. Choice is the headwater of responsibility. Choice is when you say 'I will' or 'I won't.' Choice is when you decide 'Yes' or 'No.' And once you make an authentic choice, you immediately become responsible for the choice you made. Responsibility always begins with choice.

"Carl, take a look at where you've been successful in your life. It always began with a choice. As soon as you made a real, true choice, you became responsible. When you choose to become responsible, your relationship to that which you are responsible for is much more powerful than when you're forced to do something or have to do something."

Sidney leaned into his next words. "Choice is the headwater of responsibility. Responsibility is the precursor for commitment. Commitment leads to effective action. Effective action leads to results."

"You say it so convincingly, Sidney."

"That's because I am convinced. I know this works."

"Will it work for me?"

"If you really understand the concept, it will. So, tell me what you think you need to do."

Carl thought for a few moments. "I need to have my staff choose to be accountable about their jobs. This should lead to them being more responsible, which in turn heightens their sense of commitment. And being more committed means they will take effective action which will ultimately produces positive results."

"Very good!" Sidney grinned. "I think we have a winner."

"You sure I didn't cheat?"

"Not you, Carl. Your core values are in the right place for a dentist."

"Where's that?"

"Your mouth."

TWENTY-EIGHT

Hold to Account

SEEING THAT THEY WERE MAKING good progress, Sidney pressed on. "If you have people who are responsible, then you can create a management system that empowers them and drastically reduces your time as a manager."

"I'd love that," Carl said. "So much of my time is spent handling things I think I shouldn't have to."

"Yes, Carl, you'd have a lot more time to do those things that would keep your practice viable during this tough economy."

"Now that would be something. How do I get this going in my office?"

"I recommend management by accountability, not management by job description," Sidney answered. "Let's go back to the example of you as a parent. If I asked, 'What are you accountable for as a good Dad?' what would you say?"

"First, I'd need to know what exactly you mean by *accountable*."

"*Accountable* means this: What you can be counted on

for, always, as a parent. No matter what time. No matter what place. No matter how old your kids are. As a Dad, what can you always be counted on for?"

"I guess I'd have to say, I'm accountable for my kids' well being. That would be my bottom line."

"And if one of your kids called right now, would you take the call?"

"Of course. It could be an emergency."

"So accountability is not time or distance related. It is an *always*."

"Absolutely."

"Now, in order to be accountable, you need someone to be accountable to. You can't be a Dad without a child. You can't be an owner without a business. You can't be a coach without a player. Accountability is a relationship-based phenomenon. You have to be accountable to someone. Do you see that?"

"I get what you're saying," Carl said. "But what's the difference between accountability and responsibility?"

"Responsibility is a stand you take. You say 'I will do this' and you keep your promise. You don't need a relationship to be responsible. But with accountability you need to have a relationship with another person."

Sidney paused and saw Carl's brow furrow. "Let me give you an example, Carl. In your practice, as an owner, manager and leader, you have no one you are accountable to, except yourself. You have no one to hold you to account for what you say you'll do. If you want to let yourself off the hook about something you didn't do, you just make an excuse. But, if you had someone to hold you to account, you are much more likely to get it done."

"Well, I have to account to my wife. Veronica holds me accountable."

"When you choose to tell her," Sidney said pointedly.

Carl hung his head. "Guilty. I guess I'm just like all those politicians who hide the truth, so they won't have to be accountable."

"Exactly, or those corporate CEOs who weren't held to account by their Boards. Or the Boards that weren't accountable to their stockholders. That's what led to a lot of the mess on Wall Street. A lack of accountability."

Carl nodded in agreement. He'd lost a lot of money in the stock market because of this lack of accountability.

"So," Sidney continued, "let's look at setting up management by accountability in your dental practice. Carl, as a dentist, you have an accountability to the patient. You believe you are accountable to the patient for delivering the right dentistry at the right time, at the right cost. And the patient holds you to account to deliver a professional service."

"Yes, I can see that."

"But you don't have the same level of accountability with anyone around your leadership or ownership of the practice. That's a missing piece for you. It's crucial to how I try to help dentists. And before you leave, we can talk about how to put that accountability piece in place.

"Without someone to hold you to account, Carl, it's easy to make excuses or come up with reasons why things don't get done or results don't get produced. You know, those hundreds of excuses, justifications and reasons you say to yourself every day. If you had someone to hold you accountable, you wouldn't have let your practice slide as far as you have. With no one to hold you to account, you just hid out and hoped it would get better."

Carl reflected on Sidney's reasoning and realized that one reason he liked solo practice was he didn't have to answer to anyone. "You're right, Sidney. When things were going well, when there were more than enough patients and money, I could get away with letting things slide. But now, when results really count, I see what that's cost me. I thought this would be about my staff and not me, but I can see it has a lot to do with me — with how I manage."

"Carl, that's a vital realization. You have to see your responsibility. It should cause you discomfort. It means you're ready to take action."

"It's painfully clear that I need to do something."

"Listen, Carl, if you were in a highly successful corporate environment, you would have to report to someone who would hold you to account. Someone who would hold you to your word. Someone who would demand you have your people perform. Someone who wouldn't tolerate you being afraid to take action. And inside that relationship of accountability, you would put your fears aside and do what needed to be done."

"But I'm not in a corporation," Carl countered. "I'm the boss. If I understand what you're saying, I still have to be accountable, even though accountability requires a relationship. As the owner of my business, I can't be accountable to myself. So, who holds me to account?"

Sidney rubbed his hands together. "That, Carl, is a critical question. But before we talk about who you are accountable to, you need to establish accountability in your office."

"How do I do that?"

"Actually it's pretty simple. You establish accountability in your office by asking the following four questions of each staff member." Sidney held up a finger as he went through each of the four questions:

1. What are the core activities you are responsible for?
2. What are the expected outcomes from these activities?
3. How will your success in these activities be measured?
4. What conditions do you need in place to be successful in these activities?

Carl wrote down the four questions on his legal pad and then read back through them after Sidney had finished. Looking a bit bewildered he asked, "That's all it takes?"

Sidney chuckled. "Of course not. It's one part of the larger process of managing by accountability. To help make that point, I'm going to give you a half hour to answer these four questions about every staff position in your dental office: front desk, hygienist, assistant, every position."

"I thought my staff had to answer these four questions," Carl protested.

As he stood up to leave, Sidney retorted, "Every good teacher should try to know the answer before he asks his students a question."

TWENTY-NINE

In the Bucket

CARL WAS STILL WRITING FURIOUSLY when Sidney entered the Great Room.

"Sidney, I'm not done."

"Take it easy. Don't worry. You can finish it later."

Carl set his pen down, massaging his right hand.

"Now," Sidney began, "I recommend you give these questions to each staff member to answer at home. You've seen that it takes some time and thought. So have each staff member write down their answers and then meet with them individually. After each of you presents your answers to the four questions, then comes the hard part. You must mutually agree on the answers."

"That sounds time consuming," said Carl.

"It can be, but you and each staff member must negotiate until you have one answer that you both fully agree on. Let's say, before meeting with your assistant, you write down that she is responsible for the operatory. She gets the rooms ready, completely set up, everything wiped down, trays fully stocked and out, hand pieces ready — a fully functional operatory."

"Exactly," said Carl. "That's what I'd expect."

"And, let's say your assistant says pretty much the same thing. So you are mutually aligned on the answer."

Carl nodded in agreement.

"Next, you look at the best way to measure her in this activity. You suggest, 'Patients are seated on time.' But she says she doesn't want to be measured that way."

"Why not?" asked Carl. "It makes sense."

"Carl, her response to that is, 'I can't have patients seated on time unless you're on time in your hygiene checks. I can't be on time if you spend too much time talking to patients. I can't promise to have the patients seated on time if you vary from the treatment plan and start a different procedure."

"Sidney, you must have a hidden video camera in my office!"

"No, Carl, I've been there myself and helped a lot of dentists in the same boat. It's pretty typical, but it underscores the fact that accountability is a two-way street. She can't fulfill her accountability unless the right conditions are in place. Unless you do what you need to, she can't do what she needs to do."

"So, management by accountability in my office means everyone needs to do their jobs right so others can do theirs."

"Exactly, in management by job descriptions, all you have is a description of an individual's job. It doesn't foster teamwork. In order for your assistant to fulfill her core activity, in order for her to be a good performer, in order for her to meet the expected outcomes, she'll need to make requests of you and of the staff."

Carl looked a bit dejected. "Man, this could take months to do in my office. Where am I going to find the time?"

"You've got to make the time, Carl. And, really, it won't take as long as you think because each of your staff really has only three or four core activities. All their various tasks fit into these larger buckets which represent their core activities."

"Not sure what you mean by buckets, Sidney."

"Take your front desk for example. She makes sure all the information, whether charts or virtual, is complete. She confirms the patient by sending a post card two weeks before the scheduled appointment, and then calls 48 hours in advance to confirm. When the patient arrives, she makes sure the contact and insurance information are up to date. She checks account balances and if there is any money owed, she asks on her confirmation call for a payment to be brought. She has already submitted a predetermination and has informed the patient how much the insurance company will pay. She's checked with the back to make sure you are running on time. And she has placed this patient in the schedule so the revenues for that day are in line with the practice goals. Your front desk does about twenty-five things and it all can fall into one bucket. Carl, what would you call that bucket?"

"I see, her core activity is scheduling — scheduling for production."

"That's the idea. Every staff member should make a list of all their duties and put them into four or five buckets — just like your duties as a Dad. Once you and the staff have defined those core activity buckets, then you determine the expected outcomes, how each staff will be measured in their performance in these activities, and what conditions need to be in place to succeed. Then you have developed management by accountability."

"Sounds doable," Carl said as he scribbled more notes to himself. "Now, Sidney, how do I manage once we have all these things in place?"

"Since each core activity is measurable, you can actually quantify their performance. Best of all," Sidney said with a smile, "you can set reasonable targets and goals."

Carl leaned back in his chair. "I can see how management by accountability would work a lot better. Rather than me telling people what to do, they would know what to do. It would be more of a partnership than a boss/employee situation. I could develop some kind of reporting system for each staff member so we could look at their measures of success in each of their core activities."

"Exactly," Sidney said. "What else does this approach offer to you and your staff?"

Carl considered for a few moments before answering. "I think it would have a huge impact on staff relations. People would probably be more demanding of each other since they can't fulfill their core activities or produce the expected outcomes alone. I also think it would demand that I be a much better boss, a better communicator and less tolerant of underperformance. I see the power of it. But, I also know it would mean some drastic changes in the way I'm currently doing business. It seems overwhelming."

"Listen, Carl. This is a lot to take in. My intention is to give you an overview this weekend, not take you through a step-by-step restructuring of your practice. Much of this information is on my website: Valuocity.org. It has samples of things we've talked about: core values, core value behaviors, examples of accountabilities. When you leave, I'll give you your own password and you can access the site any time you want. That should help as you start the process of remastering your practice."

Carl couldn't help but smile. Sidney was giving him both the push and pull he needed to remaster his practice.

Sidney looked at his watch. "It's a little after noon. Let's take a break and meet in the kitchen for lunch at 1:00. Does that work for you?"

"Sure, I could sure use a stretch. Thanks for hanging in there with me."

Sidney pointed to his coffee mug which read:

Valuocity: You Can't Fail When You Base Your Practice on Your Values

"Remember, Carl, that's not just some business slogan. That's *my* core belief."

THIRTY

The Value of Values

THE TAOS MOUNTAIN AIR FELT GOOD. Carl enjoyed the bright sun shining down from the cloudless sky. After his session on accountability, he needed a break outside to catch his breath and process all the information. Sidney's ideas intrigued him, but he worried that even though he had taken pages and pages of notes, he'd forget how all the pieces fit together.

He found himself walking near the bunkhouse alongside the stand of pine trees. He heard a screen door slap shut and looked over to see Richard stepping off the porch. Carl raised his hand in greeting, and, somewhat to his surprise, Richard walked up to him.

"How are you, Carl?"

"Doing fine. Just need some of your premium Taos air to keep my head clear. Seems to work better than coffee."

Richard smiled. "Now, there's something Starbuck's hasn't cornered the market on. Maybe we could start selling 'airspresso' and make a fortune."

Carl smiled. Richard — Fierce Eagle Richard — was still a mystery to him. He seemed at times distant and intense, yet he had a quick wit. Carl appreciated his camaraderie just now.

"Let me show you the path to the river," Richard said.

"I don't want to take up your time."

"It's Sunday. Besides, the boss would want you to see it. It's one of the main reasons he bought this place."

Richard started off and Carl, out of curiosity, followed. Past the pine grove, they followed a rocky path down a steep slope. As they made their way down the switchback trail, Carl began to hear the rush of water. He caught glimpses of the river through car-sized boulders the trail snaked around. The path finally leveled out and Carl found himself on the bank of a fast flowing river some twenty-five yards across. The unfiltered sunlight made the swirling eddies dance in mesmerizing patterns. They both stood in silence.

Carl took a deep breath. "It's beautiful."

"This river is a branch of the Rio Grande. The headwater of the Rio begins on our land and this is a small branch of the great river. Further up the mountains in a steep gorge, this river has its beginnings. It is a sacred place. It holds many spirits." Richard turned to look directly at Carl. "My tribe and my native brothers everywhere, we all have the same values. We value the earth. We value the water. We value the animals. We value the elements. Our beliefs are all about honoring these values. Our stories are all about our values. We reinforce our values in everything we do, in all our ceremonies."

Carl nodded, thinking, *Why is he telling me this?*

As if in answer to his private thought, Richard continued, "Carl, this place is sacred to me because of who I am. I am a Taos Pueblo Indian. What you see before you is one of my core values."

Richard looked out at the river again, "If you lose your values, you forget who you are. Our tribe has been here forever. We are the only Indian tribe who was never moved. We have always lived on this land. Our values have sustained us for our entire history. We value each other, we value our families, we value our children, we value our elders, we value our tribe, we value our ancestors, we value our land, and we value our sacred spirits. These values have kept us alive and taught us who we are.

"We have been a poor people and we have lived in a pueblo where at times there was little. We have had our problems with drugs and alcohol. We have had our squabbles and fights. But we are a people who have been here for centuries and will be here for many more, all because we honor our values."

The roar and rush of the river seemed to punctuate each of Richard's points.

"Carl, many people come to the ranch hoping Sidney will 'give' them the answers. But he can no more give them the answers than he can give this river to them. He can only help people understand what they value."

Richard turned back to Carl. "Once you know what you value, you must surrender to them, honor them and live by them. That's what Sidney believes. That's why I work for

Sidney. He does not tell me what to do or believe. We share common values. That's why things work so well around here."

Carl looked beyond Richard to the river, part of the headwater of the mighty Rio Grande. In such a place as this, how could one not understand the majesty of a world in which people shared a common vision?

"Yeah, Richard, I think I see what core values can really do. It'd be nice if everybody shared the same ones."

"No," Richard said plainly. "Not just the same ones. This river may mean nothing to a person who grew up on the banks of the Amazon or Nile or Mississippi. It is about respecting what people value. That's why Sidney makes a difference. He is a person who understands the value of values."

They stood silent for a moment. The river flowed by, unaware of their thoughts.

"Carl, you hungry?" Richard asked unexpectedly. Not waiting for an answer, he turned back up the path.

Carl was left standing by the river, not knowing what to make of Richard. He was every bit the teacher Sidney was, but three times as inscrutable. Finally, Carl surrendered — to his appetite — and scrambled up the path after the receding form of Fierce Eagle.

THIRTY-ONE

Do I Get Paid for This?

DAWN WAS LAYING OUT SANDWICHES, sliced in half, on a large dark green serving platter when Richard entered the kitchen with Carl trailing close behind, breathing heavily. Richard gave his wife a little hug and asked, "When will you be home today?"

"Around six. Why?"

"Remember, I have to drive Carl to the airport about five. But, I'm heading out now to practice drumming with Robert and Clarence for the Corn Dance on Friday."

"No problem. I'll get home to feed the kids and Mom, and we'll see you when you get back."

Richard squeezed Dawn's hand gently. He picked up a turkey club sandwich and wrapped it in a napkin. "Talking with mid-Westerners gives me an appetite!" He looked over at Carl, winked and left.

Just as Richard went out the kitchen door, Sidney came in and took a seat at the nook. "Sit down, Carl, we've only got this afternoon, and we still have a lot of ground to cover."

"That's what's worrying me. I'm not sure I can remember half of everything you've told me. I'm likely to forget most of it even before I land in Madison!"

"You've got your notes and, as I told you earlier, all this information is on the Valuocity.org website." Sidney took a bite of his sandwich and chewed thoughtfully. "Besides, I'm hoping you've got the bigger lesson on core values. Everything else stems from that."

Carl thought about his conversation with Richard. "Yeah, I think I'm getting the picture on core values. But I've used consultants before and everything they say makes sense at the time. Then, when I'm back on my own at the practice, I can't always put their advice together in a way that is convincing to my staff."

"Don't worry about that right now. I won't leave you high and dry when you return to Madison," Sidney reassured. "For right now, try to get the big picture."

"Okay. What's our focus this afternoon?"

"Performance reviews and salary reviews."

"What's the difference?" Carl asked skeptically. "I don't think I've ever given a performance review that doesn't end without a request for a raise. They just seem to mean the same thing to my staff. What am I missing?"

"They're very different," Sidney began. "I know this area of practice management isn't easy for dentists. It's probably one of the most stressful aspects of managing a dental practice. But, Carl, it's less complicated than you think. A performance review measures how well a person is doing their job. It provides feedback and meaningful dialogue between you and your staff. It's all about their job performance."

"But I hate that process, Sidney. If I give a staff member a good review, they automatically ask for more money. If I give them a less than stellar review, they sulk around for weeks. I've tried doing performance reviews a lot of different ways and it's always a pain."

Sidney nodded sympathetically. "Remember when we discussed developing people through work? I said that staff often leave because they know when the boss cares and when they don't?"

"I remember. And I do care. But my staff still sulks and they still ask for raises."

"Carl, when you have an employee who chooses to be accountable and chooses how they want to be measured in their job, then they want feedback and want to know how they're doing. They look to you for guidance because they want their performance to improve."

"Sure," Carl retorted, "if they think it will help them increase their salary. The way my practice is going now, I can't even afford to keep the staff I have. So what good is a performance review, and how do I say 'No' to more raises?"

"First of all," Sidney began, "don't jump to the conclusion that your staff will only work hard for more money. Second, you are not alone when it comes to finding the optimum salary balance. Most dentists confuse performance reviews with salary reviews. In my former practice and here at the ranch, we never mix the two. We do an annual salary review, and it's never at the same time as a performance review. In fact, when a ranch hand is hired, we spell it out very clearly up front. We tell them they'll have an annual salary review. Also, in the first year, they'll get two or more performance reviews so we can steer them in the right direction. No pun intended." Sidney smiled at his own joke and continued. "We compensate our employees based on performance, so our performance reviews set the stage for the salary review."

"You're telling me not to lump performance and salary reviews together? How does separating them improve performance?" Carl asked.

"Carl, when you care about your staff you want them to win, don't you? If you are winning and the practice is profitable, don't you want them to make more money?"

"Sure, that's good for everyone. But how the heck do I set it up so that we all win, and it's not just about the money?"

"You have most of the pieces right in front of you," Sidney explained. "First, you and each staff member agree on and complete their core accountabilities, then you negotiate the expected outcomes and how they will be measured in each area of their core activities. We just talked about this."

Carl nodded.

"After you have their core activities and the expected outcomes for each activity, you have half of your performance review done. Next, for each staff position, you use the core behaviors you defined yesterday. These are the behaviors that support the core values. So, now you have a second measurement."

Carl felt uneasy. All he could think about was how much work this would take, and how much the staff would resist something like this.

Sidney responded to Carl's look of dismay. "Carl, I know what you're thinking. I see it on your face. You're worried about all the time and energy it will take to get this in place. On top of that, you're wondering how the staff will react."

"Exactly!"

"Listen, I have lots of experience with dentists, and I've worked through this myself when I was in practice. What I can tell you is to trust the process. It works. What you want and what you need is a systemized approach that will ensure your core values are being honored in the workplace and your employees are fulfilling their core accountabilities, right?"

"Of course. And, if the practice is profitable, I'm fine with rewarding staff with more money. You're telling me that your performance reviews can do all that?"

"No, Carl, I am not. *My* performance reviews will not work for you and no one else's will either. Only yours will. I can't just give you copies of my performance reviews. I'm guiding you to create your own. Since each individual dentist has their own distinct core values, and these core values have their own explicit definitions that unfold into core activities and into core behaviors, your performance reviews will be unique to your practice. One size does not fit all.

"Carl, your reviews will indicate very clearly if your core activities are being performed and will also measure if your staff is demonstrating the core behaviors that you have identified."

Sidney paused for his message to sink in, and then continued, "Now, repeat back to me what I just said."

Carl sat up a bit straighter, as if he'd been called on in class. "That I should create my own performance reviews and use them to measure how the staff is performing their core accountabilities and how well they are demonstrating behaviors that support the core values in the office."

"That's right. You got it. So, grab a sandwich and then complete the assignment. I want you to choose one staff person in your office and make an outline. I want you to list their four to five core activities. Then, under each core activity, list two or three expected outcomes and a metric for measuring how successful they are in the activity. Clear so far?"

"Yes."

"Then, below that I want you to list your core values, and under each of those I want you to list the behaviors that you want to see in the practice. Okay?"

"Got it."

"All right, I'll check back in an hour. Is that enough time?"

"Enough time for my head to explode."

Sidney laughed out loud. "That usually doesn't happen until we get to Salary Reviews."

THIRTY-TWO

Ready to Perform

CARL HAD MOVED ONTO THE PORCH with several sandwiches and a mug of coffee to finish Sidney's assignment. He had been working diligently for an hour when he noticed Sidney approaching, dusting himself off. He had a slow, steady, contented gait. Carl envied what he saw. Sidney seemed to be in command, to have an awareness, to be attuned to his surroundings. He was comfortable with being in charge.

Carl wondered how his staff would perceive him walking through the office these days. Was he the Captain of the Ship? Or was he a Failing Mouse?

Sidney stepped onto the porch. "Howdy, Carl. How's it coming?"

"Fine. Smoother than I thought. You might be converting me."

Sidney smiled. "I'm not going to convert you to anything. You're going to have to decide for yourself that following your core values is smarter than ignoring them."

"Do I get a ranch like this if I do? You certainly look like you enjoy everything about this place — even though it keeps you hopping busy."

"You know, Carl. Someday soon I hope you have the same feeling about your own practice that I now have about this place. The ranch and conference center are my babies. I've got some really good people working here, and they make this place hum. I couldn't do it without them. But we work together. We completely and mutually support the core values of the operation, and we know we're making a difference. I know that's what you want as well."

"That's just what I want, that sense of accomplishment and fulfillment, that confidence in what I do. That's why I came here."

"Good. Then let's get back to work. Show me what you wrote for your performance reviews."

Over the next few minutes Sidney read through Carl's work. Carl had done a nice job with the outline. He had filled in the core activities, the expected outcomes from each activity and how he would measure how successful each staff member was performing each activity. Carl had also listed the core values as well as the behaviors that demonstrated them in action.

"These look good. It looks like you're starting to understand how the performance evaluations you've created can only work for you. Giving you copies of mine or someone else's wouldn't generate the results you're after. Now, I want you to think about how you want to define the parameters on your scoring scale. How do you define a '1' and how do you define a '10' and what goes in between?"

"Well," Carl began, after thinking for a moment, "I would think a '1' represents a failure to get the job done — that none of the expected results were produced. A '10,' on the other hand, would mean that all of the expected results were produced — efficiently and with satisfaction. Everything in between would be on that continuum."

"Nicely stated. That's clear."

Carl beamed, feeling like this system was really starting to make sense. He still had a question, though. "What do I do if I have a staff member that is always producing great results and scores a lot of 10s? How can they improve?"

"Great question! That's one of my favorites. Here is what I do. In order for an employee of mine to rate a 10, the employee not only must be exceptional in their performance in a particular area, but they must also figure out how to improve in that area or task and take it to a higher level. And they must share it with the rest of the staff."

"I like that idea. Mind if I borrow it?"

"Not at all. 'Borrow from the best' I always say." Sidney gave Carl a wry smile. "Okay. You just need to add a few more things and you'll be close to having completed your first evaluation. You'll also need to add sections for *Actions to Take* and *By When*."

Carl marked the titles in his notes. "Those sound like the Requests/Promises technique you used during your meeting with the ranch hands yesterday."

"Exactly. But here's how they work in the performance

review. The purpose of the performance review is to provide positive feedback on the work the staff is doing. Before the review you'll ask your staff to rate themselves on each item and then you'll rate them. After that you'll sit down together and compare your answers. And you'll ask the question: *What do you need to do to improve in this area?* You're going to write down their answers in the form of *Actions to Take* and *By When* the actions will be completed."

Carl wrote down Sidney's instructions. "So, the idea is to use the Requests/Promises technique in order to be more collaborative rather than dictatorial."

Sidney nodded. "That's the ticket. You are working with them to improve, not dictate how they will improve. Now, at the bottom of your page add the line *Goals for the Next Six Months*. That's so you can continue to develop your staff and allow them to grow in new areas."

Carl wrote *Goals for the Next Six Months* under the core behaviors. "I like this idea of goal setting and having staff figure out how to get better. That's much smarter than me trying to work out how to improve everything they do. I have a hard enough time keeping up with the technical side of my dentistry."

"That's what it's all about. Having them self-assess and work on continual improvement." Sidney reached out and tapped Carl's notes. "Just one more thought to keep in mind. This is *your* review process, and it should be modified as you and your staff change and grow. Redo the form and improve it as you need to. It is not set in stone. When accountabilities or the measurements change, change the form. This is a fluid communication tool, and it can — it should — evolve over time."

"That's good to know," Carl said. "Based on that, I think I'll add a couple lines to sum up my overall impressions of the review for the employees and let them know what I appreciate about them. I don't think I do that enough to let them know what they are doing right. I just catch myself complaining in my head, so this will help me acknowledge their contributions."

Carl added another line below the goals section that read: *Conclusions of this Review.*

"Nice touch, Carl. Acknowledgement is a cornerstone of building loyalty. Is there anything else on this topic?"

Carl looked up slowly, eyebrows furrowed, searching for a thought. "Yeah, I wrote something down — a question I wanted to make sure that I asked you. Hold on while I find it."

Carl flipped through his notes. "Here it is. You told me that performance reviews are not the same as salary reviews. I understand the link between core activities and core behaviors. How to measure them in the office. How to set this up so the staff sees this as a positive rather than a negative. But what makes the salary review process different?"

"Believe it or not, Carl, it is as simple as the performance review. The salary review, in essence, is really a second performance review. Just like the first performance review, you rate their performance, from the time of the last performance review to the salary review, with the same kind of numerical score. And if the staff member is performing well and if the practice can afford raises, they can earn one. Simple as that."

"Simple?" Carl's eyes widened as he moved forward in his seat. "Sidney, you mean to tell me that even if they are doing a great job, but there's no money for raises, they don't get one? Won't that create a mutiny? I mean they expect a raise every year. Do you have any idea how upset they'll be?"

"Carl, I can't promise you a practice without the occasional upset. We've discussed communication tools to handle upsets. You have to deal with upset people all the time in life. What I can tell you is that unless you are profitable, unless the practice, like any other business, is on target with income and expenses, you can't give people money you don't have. In this economy, most people are grateful to be working and keeping their jobs. If you're up front and honest, they'll understand. They may not like it, but they'll understand that the business must survive."

"Seriously? They won't be upset?"

"See this, Carl?" Sidney pointed to the word *Valuocity* on the coffee mug by Carl's chair. "Remember, you can't lose when you abide by your values. Owners need to make the tough decisions, and it is reassuring when the tough decisions are fully in line with their core values. Think about this for a moment. Which of your core values would be honored by being straight with your staff and not giving raises if you can't really afford them?"

Carl paged back through his notes. "Let's see… Integrity, because I would be keeping my word to do the right thing for the practice. Courage, because I would be facing my fears about communicating the truth. Respect, because I would demonstrate my respect for my staff by being honest. Excellence, because I would be doing my best to keep the practice strong and viable. Improvement, because I need to make changes to operate in the new economy. Service, because we need to remain in practice to serve our patients. And Profitability because if we are not profitable we can serve no one."

"You are definitely starting to internalize the power of your core values, Carl."

"When I look at staff raises through the lens of my core values, I see that your motto speaks volumes. If I'm true to my values, then I'm true to myself and what I tell my staff is authentic. And that's tough to argue against," Carl admitted.

"Exactly. Most breakdowns in communication and trust are a result of people sensing hypocrisy or a lack of genuine concern. Now, let's move onto the final part of the Salary Review Process."

Carl held up both hands. "Wait. If this is going to make my head explode like you said earlier, can't I at least have a final request?"

"Sure, what is it?"

"Something I value. Something that makes hard work like this easier to swallow."

"And what would that be?" Sidney asked.

"A cold beer."

THIRTY-THREE

Beer View Mirror

SIDNEY CAME BACK ONTO THE PORCH with a tray that held two frosty mugs, two bottles and a covered dish. He handed Carl a mug and a bottle. "It's Raison D'Etre made by Dogfish Head Brewery, a great little company that really follows its core values in making unique hand-crafted beers. You'd be amazed at where following your core values can lead."

They poured their beers. Then Sidney uncovered the dish on the tray to reveal a plate heaping with what looked like onion rings. But the hint of cinnamon followed quickly behind as Carl looked up questioningly at Sidney.

"Mexican Churros! Nobody does them better than Dawn. She saw me grabbing the beers and sent these along. She didn't want you to leave the ranch without sampling one of her specialties," Sidney acknowledged with a hint of pride.

"Sidney, your staff is amazing. I've been to some very nice hotels over the years for dental conferences, but the service here at the ranch has been just out of this world."

"Thanks, Carl. I'll pass your compliment along. It's one of the metrics we use in evaluating our service at the ranch here."

"What metric?" Carl asked.

"We count compliments from guests. It's a simple metric, but when you pay attention to how our guests react to our service, we learn a lot. And part of the conference center staff's annual bonus is based on this score."

"You actually keep track of compliments?"

"Carl, a lot of times, businesses — and not just dentists — fail because they don't figure out how to measure for success. If you don't take the time to determine the metrics that are essential for your business, you never know if you're gaining or losing ground."

Carl took a long draught of his beer as he considered Sidney's words. He wondered what it would be like in his own practice if he tracked compliments and complaints, on-task and off-task behaviors. He didn't want to treat his staff like they were machines, but he was beginning to formulate some metrics he thought might be worth giving a try.

"Well, I think you're onto something special with the way you measure performance around here, Sidney. And I'll give you one more measurement to consider."

"What's that, Carl?"

"Ten."

"Ten?" Sidney asked, eye brows raised.

"This beer. Definitely a ten!"

THIRTY-FOUR

Practice Success

SIDNEY LAUGHED HEARTILY. "Glad you like the brew. I think it rates a ten as well."

"It's the kind of measurement I can sink my teeth into. Like these Churros." Carl took a bite. "Tell Dawn these are a ten too — and give her a raise!"

"Perfect," Sidney said, "because that's how we are going to wrap up your stay. We're going to address salary issues. Turn to a blank page and label the top *Salary Review: Assistant*. Then I want you to write in the exact same titles you have on the performance review."

Carl did as Sidney directed.

"Now I want you to transfer the same information from the performance review to the salary review. All of the Core Activities and the list of Core Behaviors should be identical in the vertical column."

Carl quickly transferred his core activities and seven core behaviors to the new sheet. "Done," he said.

"Okay, now add a third area below Core Behaviors. Label it *Practice Success*."

Carl wrote it down and then said, "Practice Success. I guess that's the real bottom line."

"Indeed it is. Now, let me ask you: how do you determine if you're having a successful year?"

After considering for a moment, Carl answered, "I look at the collections and the production numbers mainly."

"Yes. Those are important numbers. But how do you decide if your numbers indicate success?"

"Oh, I see what you're asking. Every year I create new targets for the practice. I set a collection and production target, budget, new patient and case acceptance targets. Actually I have quite a few targets."

"Exactly, Carl. Now I want you to take a minute and think about how you can use any or all of your targets to determine if you are being successful."

"Well, I certainly want to make my targets."

"Of course you do. But what will you use to define success? Does every target need to be met 100%?"

"Well, no," said Carl reflectively. "I would consider the practice to be successful if we made our revenue targets 100%, and I would consider us unsuccessful if we were only at, say, 85%."

"Good, now you have a rough outline to work with."

"Why is that important to know, Sidney?"

"Well, in the last piece of the salary review process you must define practice success the way you want it, exactly. Then, if both collections and overhead spending, or whatever you use, are meeting targets at levels you determined earlier, then raises are possible. If targets are not being met, then no raises can be given until these measures are back on track. That's how I did it in my practice."

"So, if the practice wasn't doing well, you didn't do any salary reviews?"

"Correct. When I was in practice, my raise policy stated that very clearly. Also, part of the salary review process must consider how successful the practice is when a raise is given. If the practice is 100% successful that must be factored into a raise. If the practice is 90% successful that should be factored in as well. Why should staff get the maximum possible raise if the practice is not 100% successful at achieving its targets?"

"Boy, that makes perfect sense, though I'm not quite sure how I would do that."

"It's pretty straightforward, Carl. You determine a minimum number for which you will extend raises. Let's say you decide there will be no raises if the practice has not achieved at least 95% of its target numbers for collections. Then, come salary review time, when you look at the numbers and discover that you are only at 88%, there are no salary reviews. You might also include overhead numbers as well and look at 'net' collections number. Make sense so far?"

"Yeah. You're saying if I establish 95% as the minimal acceptable level for practice collections in order to give out raises and the practice is at less than that, then there are no raises. And if the number is, say, 96%, then staff gets raises, but maybe only at 96% of the maximum possible raise? Is that where this is headed?"

"That's the idea. Now you can see there are three separate parts that play into staff salary raises and they all have to be considered together." Sidney raised his fingers as he numbered off the pieces. "1) Performance of Core Accountabilities/Core Activities, 2) Performance of Core Behaviors, 3) Success of the Practice."

Carl wrote them down in his notes, and then Sidney continued, "Now that you have the tools to evaluate these three areas, you need to decide how to weight each."

"How do I weight them?"

"Think about the three areas you are evaluating. Do you believe that they should all carry equal weight in determining raises, or is any one area more important than another? For example, should they all be weighted 33.3% each or should the importance of each be distributed differently?"

"Give me a second," Carl said, looking down at his notes. "Well, it's critical that the practice is doing well, so I guess the most important thing would be that each staff member is fulfilling her core activities."

"Then what percentage of 100% would you assign to fulfilling core activities?"

"Well, how about 50%?"

"Sounds reasonable. How would you then weight the remaining 50% between the categories of core behaviors and practice success?"

"I'd say equally. 25% to core behaviors and 25% to practice success. Though I still have no idea how this will work."

"Patience," Sidney counseled. "We've got three areas you're using to evaluate staff. You've got them weighted in terms of importance to you and the practice. Now, this is where it gets a little complicated, so stick with me. Look at the Core Accountabilities and then look over at the list of Activities to Measure. Add up the number of activities that you are measuring. How many are there?"

"I have five."

"So, you've got five activities to measure and each has a maximum score of 10 points. So the maximum possible score is 50, right?

"Yes."

"And you have seven core values (behaviors) that you will measure worth 10 points each. That will give a maximum score of 70. Correct?"

"Okay, I'm starting to get the idea here."

"Carl, I want you to put in 50 for the maximum total points that can be achieved for Core Activities and 70 for the maximum total points for Core Behaviors and just for the sake of understanding how this works, lets project 12 months into the future and envision that the practice is in better shape and that you will be able to afford raises. Now, you said that you would weight practice success at 25%. If the practice was moving in the right direction what number would you like to pick to reflect the degree of practice success in the coming 12-month timeframe?"

"Well, if we were improving and the overhead numbers were steady, maybe I would call the practice successful if we hit 85% of targets. Does that work?"

"Sure. I just need a number for this example, but I like to see that you are now considering the overall success in the practice as a measure that must be calculated. You can see that when you put the numbers into our spreadsheet you're going to end up with a final number that represents an exact percentage of the maximum raise each staff member is able to receive based on their core behaviors, their core activities and the success of the practice."

"That's pretty slick, Sidney. I don't know how they could argue with that."

Just then Dawn appeared in the doorway. "Excuse me, Sidney. Sorry to interrupt, but it's 3:30, and Richard will be picking Carl up at five. Just wanted to make sure you're aware of the time."

"Thank you, Dawn. Thanks for keeping us on schedule."

"How'd you like the Churros, Carl?" Dawn asked.

"Outstanding! Can I wrap some of these up and take them on the plane?"

"No need," Dawn said. "I've made you a little Taos care package you can take and share with your family."

"That's so kind. You really didn't need to go to the trouble."

"It's no trouble. It's who we are around here." She shook a scolding finger and teased Sidney. "Haven't you taught him anything about core values, or have you just been drinking beer all weekend?"

Sidney laughed. "We're getting there, if we didn't have all these interruptions," he said in mock frustration.

"Well, I'll let you get back to your work. What were you discussing?"

"Raises," Carl answered.

"Oh, I like those!" Dawn winked at Carl. "Give me a few more compliments after I leave, and make sure Sidney writes them down." She walked over to the table between them and picked up the tray of bottles and mugs. With an elegant turn, she walked back into the lodge.

"She's one in a million," Carl told Sidney.

"She certainly is, and I never have any trouble figuring out her salary review. She's always at 100%."

"I'd sure like to have it that easy."

"Well, Carl, let's finish this up, so you can get on that plane tonight confident that you can make it that easy."

THIRTY-FIVE

Raising the Stakes

"REMEMBER," SIDNEY REMINDED CARL, "this whole salary review process is on the Valuocity.org website with samples you can download. All the functions are built into the spreadsheet so you don't have to reinvent the wheel."

"That sounds helpful, but I'm still a bit confused," Carl admitted. "I understand everything we just discussed, and I know I can get it from the website, but I just can't picture what this looks like. Can you give me a rough sketch, so I can work with it more on the plane ride home?"

"Of course, Carl. Actually, I've got a team working on a Valuocity Guidebook which should be ready early next year. I'll be sure to send you a copy. Give me your notebook and I'll draw a grid to help you visualize it."

Carl flipped to a fresh page and handed it to Sidney who began to sketch out a table. He put in the maximum scores possible for the Core Activities and the Behaviors and used the 85% that Carl had suggested for practice success and handed the notebook back.

"Does this make more sense now?" he asked Carl.

"Absolutely. I think I can plug in the other numbers now that I see where they go. Give me a minute to try it out. I am going to score 43 out of 50 points for Core Activities and 63 points for Core Behaviors and use 85% for practice success."

Carl used the calculator on his iPhone, copied the numbers onto Sidney's drawing and then spun the page around for him to see.

AREAS	TOTAL POSSIBLE	ACTUAL SCORE	FINAL SCORE	WEIGHT	FINAL
Core Activity	50	43	0.86	0.50	0.43
Core Behavior	70	63	0.90	0.25	0.23
Practice success	100	85	0.85	0.25	0.21
TOTAL	220	191			86.75%

"Looks good," Sidney said. "You evaluated the core activities, the core behaviors and the practice success for your staff's total score. You divided that actual score by the total possible and then multiplied each by the weight to come up with a final percentage of 86.75 which means, when you round up, your assistant scored 87%. So, in this example, since you have money for raises, based on achieving 85% of your targets, this staff member will receive 87% of the maximum available raise."

"Seems pretty straightforward, Sidney. Kind of nifty to see all we've been working on for two days reduced to a half sheet of paper." Carl took another look at the grid in his hand. "And the document on your website has everything combined into a single self-calculating spreadsheet?"

"That's right."

"So, I'll be able to see how a staff member is performing their core activities and if they are behaving in a way that reinforces the core values in the office all in one place."

"That's the idea," Sidney said.

"Plus, I'll actually have a concrete number that tells me how the practice is performing. It's a win–win if ever I saw one. How the heck did you ever figure this out?"

Sidney smiled abashedly. "Well, my definition of an expert is someone who has made more mistakes than anyone else. Believe me when I tell you I have paid my fair share of the 'stupid tax' along the way."

"Well, then I hope my next question doesn't seem stupid. How often should I do a salary review?"

"That's a vital question, but I have to answer it with another question. What does your raise policy state?"

Carl faltered. "Raise policy? Uh, I don't have an actual policy. I guess your question implies that I should. Alright, I'll add that to my to-do list. Generally, I tell new staff that I do an annual review."

"Then that's your answer, Carl. Like I said before, I recommend that you separate your performance and salary reviews and keep them six months apart."

"Why?"

"Two reasons. First, so there is no confusing the two. Performance reviews set the stage for salary reviews. The performance review communicates what needs to happen to qualify for a raise and shows how the raise is linked to performance. Second, the staff member has six months to improve their performance. The salary review measures how well they actually did improve and perform."

Carl nodded in approval. His previous system, he realized, had been somewhat arbitrary. He could see how the numerical simplicity of Sidney's system created equity and better incentives for high performance. "None of the other consultants I used in the past ever had a system like this. This alone is worth the cost of the air fare down here."

"Glad to hear it. Any other questions?"

Carl thought for a few moments. "Yeah, here's one. My full time hygienist makes much more money than anyone else, but my other staff are equally as important, maybe even more so. Do I apply the same formula to her as everyone else?"

"Carl, this is a question I'm asked a lot. This is where you have the opportunity to talk straight, be direct and make strong requests. You use the same formula for everyone including hygienists. You set their parameters for core activity performance and couple that with behaviors corresponding to their core values. This will take guts. This is why it's good to have courage as one of your core values!"

"You think my hygienist might come after me with curettes and scrapers?" Carl joked.

Turning suddenly serious, Sidney leaned forward

and said, "Listen carefully. If she isn't promoting and supporting patients to make and keep their hygiene appointments, if she isn't promoting and supporting patients to follow through with your restorative recommendations, if she isn't fully embracing and expressing the core values, if she isn't helping out assistants and the front desk in her down time, are you willing to score her low and confront her on her performance and behavior?"

"I see your point."

"Carl, many dentists complain about their hygienists but never say anything to them. They don't make direct or powerful requests. They're afraid of losing them, scared of the repercussions, worried they'll lose patients. They treat them like superstars."

Carl knew how right Sidney was as he reflected on his own practice.

Sidney continued. "Very few teams ever win a championship with a superstar. In many practices, it's the tail wagging the dog. That's one of the opportunities of this whole process."

"Opportunity?" Carl questioned. "This could cause multiple problems in my office."

"Carl, if you're one of those dentists who are tired of staff complaining about hygienists for not helping out, not completing charts, not being team players, not paying attention at staff meetings, not doing as much as everyone else, but always demanding more, then this is a golden opportunity to be a real business owner."

"I thought I already was an owner."

"Not if you let staff do things in your business that hurts it. Carl, you set the criteria for success in their accountabilities and core values behaviors. This is the best time to put your foot down about what you want and need in the practice. Are you willing to do that?"

There was a long silence as Carl reflected on what this type of ownership would mean. Did he have the courage to do it? Did he have the guts to do the right thing simply because it was the right thing to do? He felt Sidney's eyes on him.

"Don't look for an easy answer here, Carl. Are you committed to making this happen with your hygienist or not?"

"I want to," Carl responded without making eye contact.

"Can you make me a promise you'll do this?"

Carl finally looked up. "You're not going to let me off the hook on this one, are you, Sidney?"

"This is management by accountability in action, Carl. Will you make that promise?"

"Yes. I promise I'll establish this performance and salary review system in my practice — including hygienists."

"By when?" Sidney prompted. "You need to give me a time frame."

Carl closed his eyes, took a deep breath and then slowly let it out. "Within 90 days."

"I'll hold you to your promise," Sidney said. "You can

bet on it." He checked his watch. "Anything else on the topic of salary review before we wrap this up and get you on your way back to Madison?"

"Yes. One thing is bothering me about this. How do I keep my staff motivated after they get their raises? Won't they be tempted to slack off?"

"How is that different from the system you have now? If your staff is just about the money, then they might slack off. But, remember, you'll be measuring their performance more closely. You have to keep your leadership strong. You have to keep your vision, your mission, your core values in plain view — in all that you do," Sidney explained. "Then, if your targets are real, if you have a culture based on requests and promises, if you — and I mean you, Carl — are a powerful owner, leader and manager, they will respond. They will see that you are unconditionally committed to making a difference for your patients, and they will want to be a part of that."

"You mean it's all up to me?"

"Yes and no," Sidney responded.

"That's a bit cryptic."

"Well, most of it is on your shoulders, Carl, but you'll need some help."

"Such as?" Carl asked inching to the edge of his seat.

"A coach."

THIRTY-SIX

Put Me in, Coach

"A COACH?"

"Carl, as a former basketball player, you know that even the best athletes need coaches to perform at their highest levels. Tiger Woods can't see himself swing. LeBron James can't observe himself play defense. Roger Federer can't watch himself serve. Each of them has a coach. You won't find any professional who wants to get better and win who doesn't have a coach.

"A coach has a way of interacting with his or her player so they perform at their highest level at game time. A coach gets the best out of the player. A coach understands how to remove the obstacles that get in a player's way. A coach can see with the player's eyes and can actually change what the player sees. A great coach knows how to get his or her player to perform at championship level."

"But I'm a dentist, not a professional athlete."

"Yes, but you still deserve a coach. A coach has a special relationship with his player. A coach encourages, yet also demands the best and holds his players accountable. That's the most important part of what I do here with my consulting. I coach."

Carl understood what Sidney was talking about and immediately warmed to the idea. "Sidney, would *you* be my coach?"

Sidney smiled broadly. "I really thank you for asking, Carl. It means you feel I've been of value. Unfortunately, I'm not able to accept any new coaching clients right now. But, I've trained many coaches who understand my values based approach to business. You can bet they'll hold you accountable."

"Are they expensive? I'm not in great shape now, as you know."

"If you deliver on your targets and goals, if you set up and manage everything you've learned here in the last few days, if you gain more power and peace of mind, what is that worth to you?"

Carl considered how he felt when he had first met Sidney in San Antonio and how he felt so much more hopeful and in control since coming to Taos. "It would be worth a lot."

"Don't worry. You'll be able to afford it given how much your practice will turn around. Look, one role of a coach is to hold you to your word. When you come up against talking to your hygienist, your coach will hold you to your promise. You won't chicken out. You'll get it done."

"Sidney, you'll make sure I get the right coach?"

"Yes. I'll give you a couple names. These will be people

I have personally trained as coaches with long track records of winning clients. You'll wind up with a coach who has not only had their players win a championship, but consistently has them repeat as champions."

"Are you saying Phil Jackson of the Lakers is going to be my coach?"

Sidney chuckled. "Not *that* Phil Jackson, but there are a few Phil's out there, and I know most of them. I promise to make sure you find a great coach."

At that moment, Carl realized the power of a promise, the power of a commitment. The whole system of requests and promises he'd seen in action on the ranch crystallized clearly in his last question to Sidney.

"By when?"

CHAPTER 37

Pay Back to Move Forward

RICHARD SAT IN THE CAB OF HIS TRUCK with Carl's bag in the back. A warm paper bag smelling of cinnamon sat in the passenger seat next to him. Carl stood with Sidney at the entrance of the lodge, the engraved beam above them reading: *Many victories require that you first surrender.*

"I can't thank you enough, Sidney. You probably saved my practice, my marriage, and my life."

"You're the one that's going to save your practice. You're the one that took the risk to come out here. There is a line from a song that goes 'Oz didn't give the tin man what he didn't already have.' All I did was dust off the cobwebs and help you rediscover your values. You did the work. I just pointed the way."

"I wouldn't have gone anywhere, if you hadn't said something to me back on the River Walk in San Antonio. I still wonder why you did."

Sidney spoke softly. "When I was much younger, I went through a rough patch in my life. Someone I never would have suspected offered to help me. Without that person I wouldn't be here in Taos on this ranch — I might not have survived. Because of that person's help, one of my personal core values is Gratitude. This is how I try to honor that value. I try to pay it forward by reaching out to others. Like you."

"Well, I owe you for that."

"Carl, you don't owe me a thing. But if you really want to repay me you can do it by succeeding. Nothing would be more gratifying to me than if you recaptured the practice of your dreams. You can repay me by following through on the coaching. You can repay me by keeping in touch and letting me know about your successes. I ask that you check in once a month. Remember accountability is a relationship phenomenon, and for the next six months, I ask that you report to me. We'll set the time up via e-mail. That's a request. Do you accept my request?"

"Absolutely."

They shook hands, as if sealing a deal. Then, Carl got into the truck, rolled down the window, waved and shouted, "Keep a chilled beer for me. I'll be back some day!"

THIRTY-EIGHT

Homeward Bound

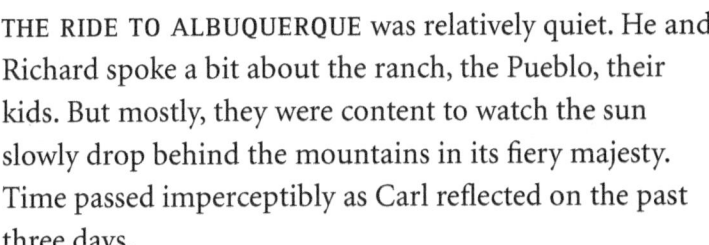

THE RIDE TO ALBUQUERQUE was relatively quiet. He and Richard spoke a bit about the ranch, the Pueblo, their kids. But mostly, they were content to watch the sun slowly drop behind the mountains in its fiery majesty. Time passed imperceptibly as Carl reflected on the past three days.

Richard pulled up to the departures curb at the airport. As Carl turned to thank him, Richard said, "Carl, before you leave I want to tell you a story that has been told in the Pueblo for generations."

"Sure."

"A young boy from the Pueblo found an eagle egg and he put it in the nest of a prairie chicken. The eagle hatched and thought he was a chicken. He grew up doing what prairie chickens do — scratching the dirt for food and flying short distances with a noisy flutter of wings. Gradually this eagle grew old and bitter.

"One day he and his prairie chicken friend saw a

beautiful bird soaring on the currents of air, high above the mountains.

"'Oh, I wish I could fly like that!' shouted the eagle. The chicken replied, 'Don't give it another thought. That's the mighty eagle, the king of all birds — you could never be like him.' And the eagle didn't give it another thought. He went on cackling and complaining about life. He died thinking he was a prairie chicken."

Richard paused for a few moments and then said, "Carl, my advice: Don't surrender to the prairie chickens."

Carl nodded his head, and they shook hands. He grabbed his laptop, the bag of Churros, got out and retrieved his carry-on from the bed of the truck. Then he went back to the passenger door and leaned in the open window.

"Richard, thank you. I promise not to listen to the prairie chickens."

Richard gave him a smile and a thumbs up. Carl turned and headed for the sliding glass doors and entered the airport. He felt Richard was right, that he actually might be more of a Fierce Eagle than a prairie chicken — or Failing Mouse.

After checking in at his gate, he sat down and took out his phone. He dialed home.

Veronica picked up on the first ring. "Hi Honey!"

"Hi, Beautiful. I'm at the airport and I'll be home by eleven."

"Great. I've missed you. Was it worth it? Did you find it valuable?"

Carl thought about the word *valuable*, what Sidney had taught him about core values and sticking to them. He felt confident that he could now weather the economic storm that had threatened his practice. He had to, because what he valued most depended on it: his family.

"Yes. It was invaluable. Everything's going to be okay — that I can promise you!"

DR. MARC B. COOPER

Dr. Cooper is President and CEO of The Mastery Company. He has been a consultant to the health care industry for nearly 25 years—at the practice management level as well as at corporate and organizational levels. Prior to his consulting career, Dr. Cooper was an academician, basic science researcher and practicing periodontist.

His consulting clients have included more than 2,000 dentists practicing in solo, partnered and group practices and their corresponding support staffs. Dr. Cooper has also worked with senior executives, managers and supervisors in large health care systems, regional and community hospitals, third-party payers, clearinghouses, biotechnical firms, information technology companies, IPAs, PPOs, DPMs and DHMOs.

Dr. Cooper focuses the majority of his work on dentists in private practice, training and coaching them to achieve mastery as leaders, managers and owners who are able to consistently operate their dental practices as successful businesses.

DR. MARK E. SILBERG

Mark E. Silberg D.M.D. has been in private practice since 1980. He is the leading dental implant and periodontal practice in Pittsburgh, Pennsylvania. Dr. Silberg is a former assistant clinical professor at the University of Pittsburgh Dental School and at Children's Hospital of Pittsburgh. He was a consultant to the Pittsburgh Zoo and is the founder and Director of the Discovery Study Club.

Dr. Silberg completed the Consultant's Training Program with MBC Consultants in 1993 and is a frequent lecturer on clinical dentistry and practice administration.

ABOUT THE TAOS PUEBLO

I chose the Taos Pueblo in Northern New Mexico as the setting for this fable because I have spent time there and became close friends with Robert Mirabal. Robert is a world renowned Native American musician. He was willing to open the gate for me into the Taos Pueblo culture, traditions and values. Robert, his wife Dawn, his family, his cousins, and a number of the Taos Pueblo elders helped me recognize the deeper meaning and profound nature of values. Though the 'pueblo' is not central to the story, the tribe's deep beliefs and values are. My experiences there contributed mightily to solidify my thinking on core values and how critical it is to weave them into the fabric of a dental practice. I deeply thank Robert and the Taos Pueblo for sharing their core values and, in the process, deepening my own.

Dr. Marc B. Cooper
The Mastery Company

VALUOCITY II

In the sequel to VALUOCITY, Dr. Carl Oldquist returns to Madison after a breakthrough learning experience on Sidney Kaprov's ranch in Taos. Sidney, a seasoned practice management coach, has shown Carl how to revive his dental practice with a renewed commitment to his core values. Carl leaves the ranch looking forward to establishing management by accountability and using Sidney's system of requests and promises to foster true excellence in his staff.

However, when Carl returns to his office, he faces immediate challenges. Members of his staff are resistant to the values-driven changes he seeks to make. On Sidney's recommendation, Carl signs on with a coach, Francis (Frank) Salvatore. Frank guides Carl methodically in confronting specific management issues and generating breakthroughs in practice performance and results. He also coaches Carl masterfully to confront his staff head on and initiate effective actions to lift his practice from near-collapse to the highest level of success.

ONE

Kiss and Tell

THE TAXI DROPPED CARL AT HIS DRIVEWAY. It was almost 11 PM. The night was damp and cold, but he stood outside for a moment staring at his house, thinking that he'd only been gone to Taos for the weekend, yet everything looked different. The neighborhood, his house, it all appeared stable and reassuring. Peaceful.

When he'd left on Friday he'd been afraid that all he'd known here in Madison might disappear because of his nose-diving dental practice. He'd tried to ignore the recession, hunkering down and hoping things would turn around on their own. That hadn't worked. The thought that he might lose his practice, his home — maybe even his family — had left him professionally paralyzed.

It had taken Sidney Kaprov's wake up call to make him see that the recession wasn't responsible for all his business problems. He was responsible. Carl Oldquist, 49-year old dental practitioner, husband and father of two, was ultimately responsible. He'd learned that on Sidney's ranch in Taos, and he was ready to own up to what he needed to do to transform his practice, to remaster his sense of ownership, leadership and management.

So, as he looked up the driveway at his house, knowing that nothing had changed in terms of his financial problems, he felt changed. He was looking differently at his situation. He felt empowered — even courageous. With lightness in his steps, he carried his suitcase up to the front door and quietly let himself in.

Veronica was there. She'd fallen asleep on the couch in the living room. Carl stood quietly and watched her for a moment. Dark hair draped lightly over her cheek, she breathed quietly, peacefully. Looking at her, Carl was taken back to a moment earlier in the day when Sidney's ranch foreman, Richard, had shown him a place on the river that was sacred to his people. Richard had explained to Carl that the core values of his people were tied up in the setting of Taos. The land, rivers and mountains were their context. Their anchor. Their beliefs.

Carl had gotten a sense of Richard's commitment to Taos and to his Pueblo ancestry, but now, watching his wife, he understood more fully what core values meant. Veronica and his two children were his context and he valued them above everything. He knew he had to bring the same commitment he had to his family to his dental practice. Integrity. Honesty. Communication. Excellence.

With those thoughts in mind, he bent down and gently kissed Veronica's cheek. Her eyes fluttered open. "Carl," she whispered drowsily, "I didn't hear you come in."

"I missed you," he said, sitting on the edge of the sofa. "I missed you something fierce."

Veronica sat up and scooted close. "Oooh, is that 'Taos

talk' again? I kind of like it. You sounded so much more relaxed when I talked to you at the airport. Did things go that well?"

"Better than I expected. There's a lot I need to do, but I feel like it's all doable now."

She put her arms around him. "What changed?"

He looked Veronica in the eyes for a long moment, something he hadn't done for months, and then took her in his arms.

"I did," he said.

She smiled. "Tell me all about it, handsome!"

He kissed her. And told her everything.

TWO

The Poisoned Well

THE NEXT MORNING, Carl arrived at his dental office twenty minutes earlier than usual. He keyed in the alarm code and watched as the small light on the metal plate moved from red to green. He wanted to be the first one in the office. Both to collect his thoughts and set a good example.

He sat down at his desk and pushed aside a small stack of unfinished charts. Several sticky notes with names and phone numbers were stuck to his computer screen. Monday's day sheet was printed out, resting on the right-hand corner of his desk as it always was. He checked his e-mail and scanned three communications accompanied by radiographs from specialists, two from endodontists and one from the oral surgeon. Then he got up and walked to the front desk.

He wrote Sharon, his office manager, a note that he wanted to have a full staff meeting at lunch and asked her to put it on the schedule. He also asked her to order pizzas and be prepared to hear about what he'd learned from his trip to Taos. Carl would make the announcement about the staff meeting at the morning huddle. He was eager to get his staff excited about the changes Sidney had inspired him to make in the practice.

After putting the note on Sharon's phone, Carl returned to his private office, located right behind the reception desk. His office had two doors. The door to the right of his desk led to the hallway where the five operatories and a small lab were located. The door directly across from his desk opened onto the reception area. Often he left this door slightly ajar so he could hear what was happening at the front desk.

Leaning back in his leather chair, Carl reviewed his Taos notes. On his flight home, he'd tried to map out what he would say. He wanted to be clear about what changes would be implemented in the practice and how he and the staff would go about it. He penned some ideas on how he would approach today's staff meeting. As he wrote, he remembered the excitement he felt when talking to Sidney about using core values to redefine the practice. He was convinced a values-based approach would really re-energize and inspire his staff.

Carl heard the front door open. Sharon, his office manager and Karie, the lead assistant, came in chatting.

"I must have forgotten to turn on the alarm before I left on Friday," Sharon said. "Oh well, it wouldn't be the first time."

"Isn't Dr. Oldquist back today?" asked Karie.

"Yes, and you know how he is after one of these consulting sessions. All excited like a kid. Don't worry, though, after a few days it'll all wear off and everything will be back to normal."

"But Sharon, everyone knows the practice isn't doing very well. Before he left Dr. Oldquist was really worried. There were hardly any new patients last month and we're having trouble filling both his schedule and the hygiene schedule."

"Well, whatever he got in New Mexico isn't going to work. He should listen to me. I've been doing this for 12 years. I know this practice. I know the patients. I know what needs to get done."

As Carl listened, he could feel his resentment growing. Sharon had been with him a long time, and yes, she knew the patients and the systems. She knew her job. She did her job, but she also caused trouble on a regular basis.

Sharon bossed people around. Staff often complained about her. She didn't answer Carl's questions directly. She wasn't very open to his requests. She was resistant to change. Many times Carl had an idea about what to change in the office and brought these thoughts up at staff meetings, only to have Sharon say, "That won't work."

Sharon knew the patients, knew about their families, knew about them personally. She knew how to schmooze them. And she was a fixture in the community. On a certain level, Carl was afraid to confront her. She had a lot of power in his practice — maybe too much.

Sharon was the highest paid employee nearing $72,000 a year — not including her health benefits and a matching 401K plan. She only worked a four-day week and rarely, if ever, came in on her days off. Carl couldn't remember ever seeing her in on Friday when he was there catching up on his charts, making his calls to the lab or fixing equipment.

With benefits and taxes, Sharon was a six-figure employee. But, did she bring in any new business for the practice? Did she manage the schedule and the patients so they were productive enough to pay the bills? Did she market? No. Not much. Never.

Carl felt now more than ever that Sharon was taking advantage of him and, hearing her declare that nothing was going to change, upset him. The weekend at Sidney's Values Ranch suddenly became a distant memory, as all the usual management issues and office politics rained down on him. His certainty in core values was losing ground in the torrent of his frustration.

He knew the staff meeting at lunch would be a failure. Sharon had already poisoned the well.

ORDER FORM

Fax: (603) 720-0369. Send this completed form.

Telephone: (425) 806-8830. Have your credit card ready.

Postal: Sahalie Press, PO Box 1806, Woodinville, WA 98072

Online: http://www.Amazon.com

Email Contact: info@MasteryCompany.com

Guarantee: I understand that I may return any book for a full refund — for any reason, no questions asked.

- ☐ *Mastering the Business of Practice* ($19.95)
- ☐ *Partnership: Why Some Succeed and Why Some Fail* ($13.95)
- ☐ *SOURCE: The Genesis of Success in Business and Life* ($11.95)
- ☐ *Running on Empty* ($11.95)
- ☐ *VALUOCITY: A Fable for Dentists* ($12.95)
- ☐ Subscription to the **Mastery Newsletter** (FREE)

Name: _____

Shipping Address: _____

City: _____

State: _____ **Zip Code:** _____

Sales Tax: Add 8.9% sales tax for products shipped to Washington State, USA.

Shipping by Air: U.S. $5.00 for first book $2.00 for each additional product.

Payment: ☐ Personal Check
☐ Credit Card (Visa, MasterCard or Amex)

Card Number: _____ **Exp:** _____

Name on Card: _____

Billing Address if different from Shipping Address above:

_____

_____

_____

www.ingramcontent.com/pod-product-compliance
Lightning Source LLC
Chambersburg PA
CBHW020647220526
45464CB00001B/322